11-7-67
2-9-68

RAILS
SAGEBRUSH
AND PINE

RAILS SAGEBRUSH AND PINE

A Garland Of Railroad And Logging Days
In Oregon's Sumpter Valley

By Mallory Hope Ferrell

Golden West Books

San Marino, California

ACKNOWLEDGMENTS

For their cooperation in the preparation of this tribute to Sumpter Valley Days, I am indebted to many. For assistance in gathering photographs for a 70 year period, I thank Richard Kindig, the late Lucius Beebe and his associate Charles Clegg, Fred Jukes, Al Farrow, Jack Holst, Jim Gertz, Bert Ward, Emery J. Roberts, John Cummings and Arthur Petersen, all historians and photographers of the Pacific Northwest woods. Additionally, my appreciation is extended to Warren K. Miller, D. S. Richter, Dick Datin, and Shay historian Mike Koch.

To the following former employees of the Sumpter Valley Railway, and the connecting logging lines, I thank W. A. Roundy of LaGrange, Bruce Morehead, a former Baker White Pine right hand man, Mike Walter and Claude Green, the erstwhile engineers from Baker, Marriner S. Eccles, who as a young man was charged with the construction to Prairie City, Earl Emlaw, and the late F. M. Shurtliff. These men spent hours checking detail, driving over old grades, digging into faded memories to produce vivid stories and rare yellowing photographs.

For countless evenings spent in checking rosters and other historical material in their private libraries and collections, I thank Colorado historians Robert A. LeMassena, John Maxwell and Cornelius Hauck. In addition I appreciate the courtesies of David L. Stearns, Gerald M. Best, Lillian Mendenhall, Ron Harr, and Michael Dunn III.

The artistic talent displayed on these pages is the work of Howard Fogg of Boulder, Colorado, and Virginia art director Casey Holtzinger. The scale drawings made especially for this book are the genius of H. Temple Crittenden and John Lewis, to whom go my thanks.

A special note of gratitude to three friends, all experts in their fields, for their company on trips into the Oregon wilds, their continued cooperation, criticism and trust. Brooks Hawley, that bard of Sumpter Valley who knows more about Sumpter's early mining days than any other man in the state. Brooks was always available to check just one more logging branch which twisted up just one more creek. During the years this book was in preparation, Henry R. Griffiths, one of the finest photographers of the railroad scene was a true friend. Hank's hospitality on my frequent trips to the area was unexcelled, plus his skill at copying the many faded photographs displayed throughout this work. To Donald Duke, publisher of Golden West Books, my deepest appreciation. His guidance and faith brought my life long project to reality.

Lastly, my sincere thanks to the girl who gave up many dinner parties, dances, movies and evenings out, while a busy typewriter clattered away in the den . . . my wife.

DEDICATION

To C. Walter Mendenhall and Don H. Roberts, two lifelong friends, I dedicate *Rails, Sagebrush and Pine*. As small boys they watched the narrow gauge trains pass, and as men kept alive these memories with their historical research, vast collections of data and photographs. Their deaths within months of each other were a deep loss to all those who knew them. It is my hope this book will live up to their tradition.

"Swift toward life's terminal I trend;
    The Road seems short tonight;
God only know what's at the end —
    I hope the lights are white."

— Cy Warman, Denver & Rio Grande Engineer

FOREWORD

DEEP in the heart of the Blue Mountains of eastern Oregon once stood vast stands of virgin timber, giants of the forest, covering every slope, mountain and valley with towering splendor. When the migrating loggers saw the pine and fir that grew here, they said there couldn't be timber that big and tall. And thick. Why Holy Mackinaw! The great trunks stood so close that the 'jacks wondered how a tree could be felled at all. Here was raw lumber for the taking, and beneath these roots lay GOLD!

The skidroad was the western loggers' first and greatest contribution to the science of moving timber, but in this country it was inadequate and slow. The railroad with two steel bands and strong locomotives was the only way to move logs. To this end was built the Sumpter Valley Railway, Oregon's most notable and long-lived of all narrow gauges of the Pacific Northwest, built in the age of lumber barons and *Narrow Gauge Fever*. This was an era when sawmills served up millions of board feet and sent it to market on small flat cars riding over three-foot tracks.

Born with the Stump Dodger were an array of privately owned logging concerns laid with crooked slim gauge tracks into the thick forest; they kept stables of little Shays, Climaxes and Heislers ever hot and ready to bring the logs out of the woods. The lives and organizations of these logging lines were intertwined with the growth and ownership of the Sumpter Valley, so that now they are a part of its history.

As the huge stands of timber became exhausted, thrifty loggers tore up their tracks and relaid them in a new location. The Sumpter Valley kept extending its own rails to reach the populace, there providing daily freight and passenger services. The process was repeated up and down every gulch and creek in eastern Oregon for over 50 years.

Timber was not the only asset reflected on the ledgers of the narrow gauge Sumpter Valley Railway. With the inauguration of service to Sumpter, there came a rich gold bonanza. Though short lived, it enriched the treasury of the railroad, adding color to its history. Cattle too was important. Soon after the turn of the century, cattlemen discovered the lush grass along the Sumpter Valley line and dispatched prime beef on the hoof to Portland's packing houses.

Unique in contemporary railroading was the equipment operated by the Sumpter. Locomotives and cars alike were mostly secondhand and had seen service on such legendary lines as Denver, South Park & Pacific, Colorado Central, Carson & Colorado, and the fabled Rio Grande Southern. The roster became a virtual potpourri of every known make and variety of narrow gauge equipment.

Best known Sumpter Valley locomotives were two narrow gauge Mallets designed for service on the old Uintah Railway. From the summer of 1940 on, these engines with their 2-6-6-2 wheel arrangement, created plenty of action on the Sumpter Valley's twisting grades, and were the star performers in one of the Northwest's finest steam shows. Rail photographers flocked to witness the performance, and it was no surprise to see Graphic-armed lensmen like Hank Griffith, Dick Kindig, or the late Lucius Beebe at trackside.

All is quiet now in Sumpter Valley. The decline of lumbering in the region spelled slow death for a once-happy railroad. Sagebrush and small pine are now reclaiming the old right-of-way, and yet on a winter's evening stories still flow in the warmth radiated by the stove in the Sumpter General Store. It's all just history now — that and a few faded photographs on a wall or at the bottom of a steamer trunk, a trace of right-of-way or rotting ties here and there . . . and memories.

Rails, Sagebrush and Pine is the story of a warm and unusual railroad. Here is the slim gauge Sumpter Valley Railway, its people and places, its locomotives and trains, its good life and hard times.

Mallory Hope Ferrell

July 15, 1967

TRAIN SCHEDULE

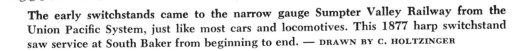

The early switchstands came to the narrow gauge Sumpter Valley Railway from the Union Pacific System, just like most cars and locomotives. This 1877 harp switchstand saw service at South Baker from beginning to end. — DRAWN BY C. HOLTZINGER

Timber And Gold Dust

THE EVENTS that led to the forming of the Sumpter Valley Railway germinated years before the railroad was even considered. The first emigrants moving into Oregon from the East in the early 1800's, paused by the present site of Baker, a sagebrush and willow lined spot where the Powder River entered the big valley. These emigrants entered the valley several miles east of Flagstaff Hill, on the old Oregon Trail, not by way of the present highway and the Union Pacific mainline. To these pioneers, who were heading for the lush and fertile lands of the Willamette Valley, there was little for them in this expanse of sage and greasewood. The Blue Mountains, towering to the west and north, were more of a barrier to be crossed in their long and tiring journey to what they hoped to be the promised land. These settlers thought little of the forested slopes or the valuable ore lying under the surface. They did pass this way, and even today the eroded wagon tracks may be seen along the route of the Oregon Trail.

Gold was not discovered until the autumn of 1861. Henry Griffin and three companions heading northward toward Walla Walla, following an unsuccessful search for the lost Blue Bucket Mine in the Malheur region of southwestern Oregon, decided to prospect along the Powder River. Here they found pay dirt, in what is now Griffin Gulch about two and one-half miles up the river from the future site of Baker, on October 23, 1861.

༄༅༄༅༄

Sumpter Valley Railway No. 2, a Brooks built 2-6-0 and caboose 02 pause in Boulder Gorge for this classic one second exposure on a glass plate negative.
— **HENRY R. GRIFFITHS COLLECTION**

As a result of exaggerated reports, a gold rush was underway the following spring. The town of Auburn, named for Auburn, Maine, sprang up almost overnight in true gold-town fashion. Within a year, eastern Oregon's first gold strike created a thriving town of 6,000, and the Baker County seat was moved there in 1862. Griffin's boom town began to wane by the end of 1864, and the seat was eventually moved to Baker City four years later.

Henry Griffin, his partners David Littlefield, William Stafford, and G. W. Schriver were soon forgotten. Gold seekers moved on to richer ground. Griffin died there in 1883 and the town of Auburn crumbled. Today, hunters walking through the powder-like soil of the abandoned town will find his grave marked by a simple stone in an obscure cemetery.

This was the scene gazed upon by young David Eccles shortly after the Civil War. Having emigrated from Scotland with his parents in 1863, he with his family settled in Florence, Nebraska. At the age of 14, Eccles walked nearly a thousand miles to Utah with a party of Mormon pioneers. David's father, handicapped by blindness, was unable to work at his trade of wood turning except by the sense of touch. The responsibility of supporting the family was placed on young David's shoulders. He often made trips to the adjacent mountains to select suitable woods for his father's work. After the wood had been converted into kitchen utensils and other items, he then took the finished goods to surrounding towns where they were exchanged for molasses, meat and other necessities.

It was not by choice but necessity that David Eccles journeyed to Oregon in 1867. From the Salt Lake Valley he started over the Oregon Trail to Oregon City, believing better opportunities lay farther west. It was during this trip he noted the vast timber resources of the Blue Mountains, although 20 years were to pass before he returned to this land. After laboring in the coal mines at Almy, Wyoming, he cut timber in the mountains not far from Ogden. In 1872, Eccles con-

In this early 1881 scene, teams bring pine logs to waiting link 'n pin cars not many miles out of Baker City. Timber came easily in this portion of the valley, but tough grades and rough logging lay ahead for the young jacks standing on these loads. Many years will pass before the timber supply is exhausted. — FLOYD CARPENTER COLLECTION

tracted to furnish logs for Bishop David James' sawmill, located on the Monte Christy, the divide between Utah and Wyoming. The following year he entered into a partnership, purchased a small sawmill and operated as the firm of Gibson, Eccles & VanNoy. The new organization not only cut timber, but opened a retail lumber yard in Ogden, where they operated a small planing mill. By 1881 Eccles became the sole owner of the Ogden mills, while operating four additional sawmills near Scofield, Utah.

In 1875 Eccles married Bertha Marie Jensen. That marriage produced 12 children. Being of Mormon persuasion, he also later took as his wife Ellen Stoddard, daughter of John Stoddard, a pioneer of 1856. This marriage of 1885 added nine more children to the family over the years. The members of the far flung Eccles family have been active in the industrial, financial, artistic and religious life of the west, entering into all phases of the country's development.

In 1889 David Eccles returned to Baker City, Oregon, and formed the Oregon Lumber Company. This firm would grow to become the largest of its kind in the state and would provide the financial backing for an empire of over 50 banking, railroad and industrial institutions with which Eccles was associated.

Baker City

Baker City had its beginnings as a town in August 1864, when R. A. Pierce, sensing that mining was on the decline in Auburn, came down from the hills. Here he laid claim to part of the land where the city was later built. Pierce named his townsite "Baker," but local residents persisted in calling it Baker City until about 1910. Both Baker City and the county were named for Colonel Edward Dickinson Baker, Senator from Oregon, who was killed at Ball's Bluff, Virginia, on October 21, 1861. About the same time Henry Griffin discovered gold several miles out of town.

The town was laid out in 1865 and the following year the Oregon State Legislature passed an act designating Baker City as the official county seat. There was a two-year delay in relocating the county seat from Auburn. This delay was due to the fact that Auburn would not yield the official records. Stage lines soon connected Baker City with the rapidly growing mining districts of Granite and Bourne to the west, and more distant cattle country. By 1874 Baker City was incorporated with a population estimated between 1,000 and 1,200. The village blacksmith, S. B. McCord, was elected the mayor and he served four terms. Other than McCord's blacksmith shop, a saloon, bank, two hotels, and an assay office, Baker City consisted of cabins. It was during this era that the county's first newspaper, the *Bedrock Democrat* was founded by former Confederate soldier, L. L. McAuthor, and his partner, M. H. Abbott. Other publications now vanished appeared in the city over the years, such as *The Reveille, The Enquirer, The Tribune, The Sage Brush,* and the *Eastern Oregon News.*

It was not until David Eccles came to town that the hamlet realized its destiny as a lumbering center.

Rail Talk

The citizens of eastern Oregon wanted a railroad. They petitioned Congress for a bill for the construction of the Northern Pacific through Oregon. This bill, presented by Senator John H. Mitchell, was defeated. The citizenry looked to the Union Pacific for help; however, the Northern Pacific controlled navigation on the Columbia River and was in no hurry to build or permit the building of a railroad. A company organized in Seattle as the Seattle, Walla Walla & Baker Railroad Company, proposed to build a narrow gauge railroad between those points, but it never got beyond the incorporation stage.

It soon became apparent that the route through eastern Oregon would go either to the Oregon Railway & Navigation Company or the Oregon Short Line, since both roads were progressing towards Baker, simultaneously but from opposite directions. A battle royal developed between the two lines for a right-of-way in the narrow canyon north of Huntington. For a while both roads intended using it, but it was proved there was room for only one. The difficulty was resolved at a joint stockholder's meeting in far off New York City in 1883. The OR&N was to build through Baker City to Huntington, and the two roads met there the following year.

A contemporary newspaper report tells of the first train through Baker City on August 19, 1884. It was only a construction train, with no big speeches, but it meant a lot to the folks of the town.

Coming Of The Rail

"There was rejoicing in Baker City today and naturally the unwonted whistle of the locomotive had music for the ears of the pioneer people. The throngs gathered at the depot to welcome the iron monster of strength and marvel of beauty as it toiled along with its load of ties, rails, telegraph poles, etc., and the quickness and exactness with which the rails were laid elicited many exclamations of delighted surprise. The train did not remain long at the depot, but pushed onward its task of making connections with the Atlantic seaboard and the world."

In 1887 the Oregon Railway & Navigation Company was leased to the Oregon Short Line, a Union Pacific subsidiary, and both lines operated as a part of the Union Pacific since 1896-7. Huntington, Oregon, is still a busy division point and giant yellow diesels still twist up the rugged, once disputed grade to Baker.

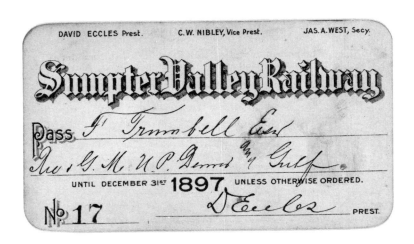

A Sumpter Valley six per cent gold bond. — EARL EMLAW COLLECTION

Rails Down The Valley

THE YEAR 1890 was a momentous one for Baker City. Making history early that spring was an effort by the Oregon Lumber Company to interest the public in construction of a proposed Sumpter Valley Railway. C. W. Nibley, lumber company president, reported to a citizens' meeting held in the First National Bank that his firm had thoroughly investigated the large tracts of timber lying between Baker City and Sumpter, and that it was this company's conclusion that it should build a railroad to tap this forest belt and build their mills at Baker City.

Nibley stated that David Eccles and the Oregon Lumber Company would put up $200,000 of necessary capital if the local citizens would subscribe to an additional $50,000 worth of stock deemed necessary for the building of the road. A committee was formed and by mid-August had raised the money, only to be notified the funds were not necessary, the lumber company having acquired the financial backing to build the road. They asked only for ten acres of land in Baker City on which to build the depot and right-of-way.

The Sumpter Valley Railway Company was chartered on August 15, 1890, with David Eccles as its president; Joseph A. West, superintendent; and a board of directors composed of Eccles, Nibley, John Stoddard, William Eccles and F. M. Shurtliff. Shurtliff's presence gave the board an unusual touch: he was a locomotive engineer on the line as well as a director.

Rail and equipment were promptly ordered for the new road, while Joseph A. West completed his survey to McEwen, the first terminus some 22 miles distant from Baker City. In the meantime, David Eccles acquired a number of shares of Union Pacific Railroad stock and through Mormon friends, exercised surprising influence over the giant rail line. His proposed narrow gauge railroad was planned at a time when the Union Pacific itself operated a vast network of three-foot gauge lines in Colorado, Utah, Montana, and other parts of the West. The Union Pacific was standard gauging many of these lines at the time. Its Utah & Northern Railway between Butte, Montana, and Pocatello, Idaho, was the first to receive such treatment in July 1887. This released some 50 odd three-foot gauge locomotives and 1,500 assorted cars. By late summer, a tiny Baldwin built 4-4-0 lettered Union Pacific and carrying road No. 285 arrived in Baker City aboard a flat car from Pocatello. The vintage 1880 teakettle was unloaded at South Baker, where a new sawmill was being built by the Oregon Lumber Company, and was promptly put to work on a construction train laying yard trackage and a portion of the mainline into the timber. All construction ceased by winter on account of heavy snows, in fact it was July 1891, before rail finally reached milepost 19. On August 1, the first car of logs rolled into South Baker behind the 4-4-0 which retained her large No. 285 on the tender.

Additional equipment obtained from Union Pacific's *Oregon Short Line and Utah Northern* consisted of 60 narrow gauge cars of all classes still lettered Union

Oregon Lumber Company's first sawmill at South Baker City shortly after the Sumpter Valley Railway started. — **BROOKS HAWLEY COLLECTION**

Against a background of imposing Oregon timber, Sumpter Valley's first Baldwin built Consolidation type locomotives are pictured in the valley shortly after the turn of the century. Logging on the main line all day near Sumpter, No. 7 puts power to the rail and is joined by No. 8 with the daily passenger. No. 7 is a former Rio Grande Southern engine, while No. 8 is fresh from the Rio Grande Western. —
HENRY R. GRIFFITHS COLLECTION

Pacific. This equipment provided the mainstay of Sumpter Valley's rolling stock during the first decade of operation. These cars kept their Union Pacific lettering and typical U.P. white facia strips for many years.

Tracks reached McEwen by October 1, and a depot was constructed. The town was named for Thomas McEwen, formerly a stage driver and later operator of stage and freight lines to Sumpter and Canyon City. Britten Station, which was located one mile away on Deer Creek was the original stage stop, but when the railhead came to McEwen the stage lines moved to the new site. Within a year the town boasted two stores, two blacksmith shops, a saloon, Odd Fellow's Hall and a Methodist church.

Baker City felt the effect of the lumber business and the new Seven Devils mining boom. In the spring of 1892, the Baker City Sampling Works was built. This plant enabled gold producers to test their ore at home, whereas formerly it had been necessary to ship it to Denver or Butte for assay.

At the same time George and Joseph Stoddard formed the Stoddard Brothers Lumber Company and built their first small mill on Clear Creek near McEwen. They logged this area with a wooden rail, mule-powered tramway, taking out the timber south of the Powder River, while Oregon Lumber Company was felling timber north of the river.

A telephone line was constructed alongside the right-of-way between the McEwen depot and connecting the Sumpter Valley Railway depot at Baker with the Oregon Lumber Company's stone office building, the Union Pacific depot and the Warshauer Hotel. This hotel had been built in 1889 by Harry and Jake Warshauer and was the most elegant public building in Baker City.

To meet the increased business demands, two second hand Brooks built Mogul type steam locomotives were purchased from the Oregon Short Line and Utah Northern's narrow gauge roster at Pocatello. These were the first of many identical 2-6-0's to serve the Sumpter Valley.

About five miles from Baker City, engineer Frank Shurtliff steamed No. 2, a Brooks built 2-6-0, across the Powder River then at near flood stage. Fireman Tom Courtner was throwing pine slabs into the firebox that day in 1898 when Shurtliff pulled on the whistle cord to signal conductor George Foster riding the shack. — ARTHUR PETERSEN COLLECTION

16

This Baldwin built American standard still carried Union Pacific lettering at South Baker in 1891. The 4-4-0 was renumbered as the four spot, later it became No. 15 and finally traded off to the Eureka-Nevada Railway. — HENRY R. GRIFFITHS COLLECTION

DAVID ECCLES 1849-1912

As soon as the track was down to McEwen, passenger service was inaugurated over the line and log trains rolled into the mill at Baker City on a daily schedule. The first printed timetable appeared in the morning *Democrat* for May 31, 1893, and stated:

"On and after June 1st 1893 the Sumpter Valley passenger train will leave Baker City at 1 P.M. and arrive at McEwen at 3 P.M. Returning it will leave McEwen at 4 P.M. and arrive at Baker City at 6 P.M. Passengers from the interior wishing to go to Portland by the Union Pacific 4 P.M. train can take the freight train at McEwen at 11:30 A.M. and reach Baker City at 2:30 P.M. —Joseph A. West, Superintendent, S.V.R.R."

Mormons

With David Eccles came many members of his faith to work in the mills, on the railroad and in the mines. A Church of Jesus Christ of Latter Day Saints was organized in July 1893, and attached to the Oneida Stake at Preston, Idaho. Its members built a chapel near the South Baker mill in 1893 and Sumpter Valley superintendent Joseph West donated a pipe organ. However, the following year the church was destroyed in a fire. Non-members employed by the

17

Sumpter, golden Sumpter was thriving during the winter of 1899-1900. The *Red Boy, Eureka & Excelsior, Golconda* and other big mines just to the north of town hammered with activity. Day was as night, and night was nocturnally noisy in this boom town.
— C. C. MCBRIDE

faith were tagged "Mormon Johns." It was only natural that these employees should dub the Mormon-owned railroad the "Polygamy Central." These phrases were used in fun and the relations between Eccles and his men were of the highest order.

Sumpter Goes Boom

Gold was discovered near Sumpter in 1862 by Hugh Asburry and four companions: John Reel, Fletch Henderson, Bill Flannigan and Dick Johnson. The five had fought under General Robert E. Lee during the early stages of the Civil War and to commemorate their loyalty to the South, named their camp Fort Sumter. Another version of the old story has it these men deserted their cause and went to California in search of gold, later migrating to the new fields of eastern Oregon. The real gold boom did not come for another 30 years, with the discovery of rich gold-bearing quartz in the upper reaches of Cracker Creek.

Sumpter is situated at the head of the valley which bears its name. The first discoveries were in placer gold in and around Cracker Creek. This stream flows through the town on its journey to a junction with the Powder River, one mile south.

There was some mining activity in the region before the arrival of the Sumpter Valley Railway on October 3, 1896, but the whistle of that first train is what signaled the biggest boom of them all. As soon as the rails were down, passenger service was extended to the new town. At the height of the boom in 1899-1901, there were two round trips a day, plus a few extras, and the two scheduled freights.

The arrival of the railroad contributed greatly to the boom. The quartz mining operations continued and huge stamping mills operated around the clock. The "Big Five" as they were called, were located on the longest continuous gold ore vein in the world, just north of the town. Today the mention of such mines as the Columbia, North Pole, Eureka & Excelsior, Golconda and Mammoth bring back memories of Sumpter's youth. The following narrative, penned in 1899 by L. Bush Livermore, perhaps best describes the boiling atmosphere of the town at the height of the boom:

"As a mining camp, Sumpter is surely it. The poetry and romance of Red Dog and Yuba Dam and other Bret Harte places in fiction and fact still remain.

"For Sumpter is wide open. It is all night. It is nocturnally noisy, it is the real thing.

"The festive faro dealer removes the limit on request. The wily stud poker professor bats his eye only when the ante touches the ceiling. The genial chuck-a-luck man smiles commiseratingly on a two-bit stake. Meals are fifty cents, beer goes for fifteen cents per taste.

"Nearly 1,500 people compose the population. Of this number perhaps half are in business. The other half is the other half— the transients, the new comer, the late goers. They are prospectors, miners, common laborers attracted by Sumpter's boom, mining men in the same class, capitalists looking for soft snaps—and finding them—curious visitors, and the rag-tag and bob-tail of humanity

Workmen had completed the new stone office building of the Oregon Lumber Co. at South Baker when this photo was made. Two narrow gauge engines and a standard gauge Union Pacific locomotive are shown. In the foreground note the postcard makers attempt to convert a standard gauge U.P. boxcar to Sumpter Valley's herald by means of retouching.

who follow whatever leads anywhere. The miners promptly find mines, the prospectors prospect, the common laborer common labors. Others coming in a constant stream— fill their places. Through all the changes, saloons, hotels, restaurants, lodging houses and dance halls reap a rich harvest. The night is the same as day. Day is intense."

With the Sumpter of Livermore's day came the inflated prices, typical of those found in many other bonanzas of the day. "The first night I spent in this town," remarked one patriarch of the hills, "I paid one dollar for a couple of quilts and a place on the floor to lay them, and was glad to get in off the streets. By dawn hammers were ringing by the hundreds and houses sometimes went up in a day." The Sumpter Valley was in a position to repay the stockholders quickly for six miles of track they recently spiked down from McEwen to the boom town. Fare from Baker City to McEwen was but two-bits (25 cents), but for the ride into Sumpter the price of a ticket was $1.25, an indication of the inflation set off by the discovery of high grade quartz up Cracker Creek.

During the boom the only large scale placer mining was carried on by the Chinese. The celestials could be found in large numbers on the hillsides near town, industriously digging for the precious metal. No estimate can be made of the amount of gold dust extracted, as inquiries into this delicate matter invariably brought the same reply: "Some days belly well, some days no good at all." But the soil along the creeks was quite rich and later to see a series

Tracks extended to McEwen when the above photograph was made in 1894 with No. 2, a Brooks built 2-6-0 on the head end of a passenger. — LYLE CARPENTER COLLECTION. The scene below was made the following year beside the Powder River as the daily passenger heads for McEwen. The crude water tank was soon replaced by a more sophisticated design. — RICHARD C. DATIN, JR. COLLECTION

of giant gold dredges scoring the area. Gold was even found on the Sumpter Valley's right-of-way near McEwen. The tracks were relocated into the tailings so the right-of-way itself might be dredged.

It must be kept in mind that any railroad serving a mining district often carried more tonnage into the mother lode than from it. The reason for this heavy traffic was huge quantities of mine timbers, milling equipment and various supplies used to extract the gold, to say nothing of the miners themselves. This was the case for the Sumpter Valley Railway. The railroad did carry ore, in fact it carried quite a bit of the stuff at one time or another. Flat cars were rebuilt into ore carrying vehicles for this purpose.

Almost overnight a small city sprang up and grew along Cracker Creek. Many people came to Sumpter looking for a fast buck. Most of them would not have come at all had it not been for the railroad which provided an easy ride into town. The town supported

three newspapers: *The Blue Mountain American, The Sumpter Miner,* and the daily *Sumpter Reporter.* There were five general stores, one hardware store, two meat markets, two groceries, a racket store, two bakeries, a candy and cigar store, five blacksmith shops, 15 saloons, two hotels and a fire house.

Virgin timber was sparse around Sumpter proper, and the lumber company started an extension from the rails at S Wye toward the summit at Larch. This line was built as a logging road and operated as such in the years of Sumpter's boom.

While Sumpter was not a logging town, there were several small mills operating over the years which supplied mine timbers and lumber. The first was Young & Rimbol, later taken over by Jim Stoddard's Sumpter Lumber Company in 1897 and operated for years at the end of the extension of the Sumpter Wye.

Red Light District

During Sumpter's heyday there was a special colony located on lower Cracker Creek. Here were the ladies of the night and easily identified by the familiar red lantern. On one rare occasion the women of camp were "exposed" when Nellie of the Forbidden City got enchantingly drunk and crossed the creek on a wooden hobby horse. With hair flying to the four winds, she rode up and down the street nearest the depot with the boisterous persistence of a cow poke.

The good women nearby blushed and went inside as the dizzy aphrodite on her stick horse played Lady Godiva with only a red kimono tied around her neck. The event made an impression on one small boy who was caught peeking from behind drawn draperies, for otherwise this tale might have been lost to the ages.

Teams, sweat and Peavey hooks were required to load the link'n pin 27-foot long flat cars of the Sumpter Valley Railway in the days before the steam skidder and loader came into vogue. — FLOYD CARPENTER

Pine slabs are loaded high in the tender of this little 1881 vintage Brooks 2-6-0 as she wheels the passenger train into Sumpter in 1896. One passenger car was usually left on a siding here for the trip up-country. Small Moguls handled the service on this branch run in the early days. *(Left)* These two urchins with their trusty dog greeted passengers at the Sumpter depot at the height of the boom. — BOTH ED HIBBS ALBUM-BROOKS HAWLEY COLLECTION

SUMPTER VALLEY RY. CO.

FIRST CLASS

BAKER

TO

SUMPTER

Loren Davis
General Passenger Agent

38842

The easy grades of the Powder River valley allowed for long log trains and small engines. Here No. 2 pulls 30 cars of logs near Thompson siding in the early 1890's. — D. S. RICHTER COLLECTION

Sumpter Valley Railway's No. 1 was a Brooks built 2-6-0 and it came to the Stump Dodger Line from the Utah & Northern Railroad. Here she poses in the Baker Yard with Engineer F. M. Shurtliff and fireman Jim Hunt. Note the dual gauge trackage in the 1897 scene. — F. M. SHURTLIFF

The daily westbound passenger paused for a picture in Boulder Gorge near the spot called Red Bridge shortly after 1900. This location was to remain a favorite with photographers as long as trains ran through the gorge. — F. M. SHURTLIFF The Oregon Smelting & Refining Co. smelter at the right, was not finished when this view was made at S Wye in 1903. At least one small boxcar in this scene saw service on the Denver, South Park & Pacific, while others are lettered for Union Pacific's narrow gauge Utah & Northern Railroad. — J. W. COWDEN-BROOKS HAWLEY COLLECTION

Red Bridge extended across the bubbling Powder River in the heart of Boulder Gorge. Here a mixed train handled by locomotive No. 5 pauses in 1908. By this time the Sumpter boom had burst and passenger service curtailed. Note the long string of flat cars coupled to the rear of the train. — F. M. SHURTLIFF

Sumpter Bust

There was increased hope for mining in Sumpter during 1903 when the huge Oregon Smelting & Refining Company smelter was constructed at S Wye, just south of town. The smelter began operation in 1904. Ore was brought into the plant on a siding which branched off from the four per cent grade from S Wye to Larch. The smelter continued to operate until 1908, but never quite got enough ore to stay busy very long. By this time the ebb had passed and Sumpter and her mining district were on the decline.

The town was near death before the final blow was dealth shortly after noon on a hot summer afternoon in 1917. "Sumpter, Golden Sumpter," wrote a Sumpter News Editor in 1902, "what glorious future awaits thee?" This question was to be answered 15 years later by H. E. Hendryx, editor of the *Blue Mountain American* when he reported on the holocaust which destroyed his town and newspaper. He said:

"Today Sumpter is facing the world after almost total destruction by fire. The fire started in the rear of the Capital Hotel on Granite Street, the alarm being given at 12:55 P.M. and by 4:00 P.M. every business house and a large number of homes were in ashes. The only two businesses left standing were the Sumpter Valley depot and the Government Forest Office. In all a total of 250 people were left homeless.

"From the hotel it was but a few moments till adjoining buildings were in flames, then jumping across streets until the entire burned over area became an immense furnace of flames, of which it seems to be impossible to give a word picture.

"Valiant efforts were made to fight the flames, six streams of water from the fire hose being used till forced to give way before onrushing flames. Unfortunately in the early stages three hose connections were lost at hydrants by burning and it was impossible to reach them to shut off the water. This with others that were left open so reduced the water pressure that it was impossible to do much toward fire fighting. Dynamite was then resorted to and added greatly to finally getting things under control."

This was the "glorious future" that spelled the death blow for Sumpter. Ed Hendryx ended his dispatch with a note of pride by saying, "Nothing less than the blow of a half-million dollar fire could knock us out."

Today Sumpter is a quiet, almost deserted place. A few of the remaining buildings stare out on the mountains around the town through glassless windows. These skeletons of the past seem to echo the sound of those riotous years. The ore dumps, dilapidated cabins, and piles of rock left by the gold dredge are sole reminders of the days when the camps hammered with industry and the loggers and hard rock men came to town for an evening of hard liquor and soft women.

Sumpter Valley No. 7 pauses in front of the Sumpter depot at the turn of the century. The boxcar at the left was still lettered U. P. for the Union Pacific System which operated many miles of narrow gauge throughout the West during the period of *Narrow Gauge Fever.* — ED HIBBS ALBUM-BROOKS HAWLEY COLLECTION

Sumpter Valley No. 12 at South Baker in the early days. — HENRY R. GRIFFITHS COLLECTION At the right, lobby of the Sumpter Hotel. Passengers who arrived aboard the little green cars during the boom were always welcome. — ED HIBBS ALBUM-BROOKS HAWLEY COLLECTION

The vault is all that remains of the Bank of Sumpter. The fire of 1917 dealt the final blow to the gold town. — MALLORY HOPE FERRELL In the 1911 scene below, engineer Fred Metzer and fireman Pete Fuller pose for photographs as the morning passenger behind No. 8 waits at Baker while mail is transferred from Union Pacific's train No. 18 to the narrow gauge cars. Note the mountain of pine slabs behind wooden supports in the tender which nearly double its capacity. — ARTHUR PETERSEN COLLECTION

No. 8 gets a shake down run in the snow after an overhaul in the South Baker shops. This Brooks built 2-6-0 is pictured on the straight stretch of track six miles out of Baker City in 1911. Her crew were L. D. Cook, fireman, Everett Jennings, conductor, and engineer U. S. Carpenter. — WILLIAM A. ROUNDY

CHAPTER 3

To The High Country

WHILE Sumpter was still a-booming, narrow gauge rails were being spiked down toward new timber. Ahead lay the huge and untouched forest of the high country, but in order to reach them, stiff grades and twisting trackage were required. No longer were the gentle gradients of the valley available to the survey crew. From S Wye, one mile below Sumpter proper, a long four per cent grade was built toward the summit of Huckleberry Mountain at Larch. Here a small section house was built and later, when larger engines arrived, a wye was constructed. Shortly after the logging trackage was laid down, the line was taken over by the railway company and passenger service was inaugurated.

On the downgrade beyond Larch, a high and beautifully curved trestle was built at Alder Springs, named after the mountain alder which abound in the area. The 60-foot high structure was a favorite picture stop in the early days and remained in place as long as the railroad continued to operate. A similar trestle was constructed on the grade west of Sumpter at a place known as Johnson's Jumpoff, but that wooden bridge was later filled-in after several trains left its curving 40-pound rails, with disastrous results.

Trackage into Whitney was completed on the first day of June 1901. The town was established as an Oregon Lumber Company camp; originally Clifford Station had been a stage stop, some three miles west. From Whitney, stage connections were made to such out-beyond towns as Unity, Hereford, Ironside, Eldorado, Bridgeport and Malheur, as well as to Austin and other John Day valley points as far away as Burns. Soon Whitney boasted a depot and the inevitable string of saloons for the loggers, who developed a thirst while daylighting the giant stands of white pine on Whitney Flat and the surrounding mountains.

Logging lines were built out of Whitney in every direction during the following 20 years. The Nibley Lumber Company built a large mill there in 1911-1912. Nibley's mill burned a few years later but was rebuilt and operated by Oregon Lumber Company during the Depression.

Construction gangs did not stay idle long, for in April 1903, the Sumpter Valley Railroad purchased three more locomotives from the Oregon Short Line and ordered rail for the extension over the second summit at Tipton. Heavy rock work delayed completion of the line into Tipton until June 1904. Tipton, in common with Larch, had side tracks and a wye, but it differed in that it had a full sized depot, staffed with an agent to handle the traffic from the then thriving Greenhorn mines a few miles to the north.

By the fall of the following year, the Sumpter Valley was operating into the former stagecoach stop of Austin Station. A huge Oregon Lumber Company sawmill was built beside the tracks at Austin and operated in the decade preceding World War I. Passenger trains from Baker City stopped here for lunch and the menu at Mrs. Austin's boarding house offered any thing from fresh mountain trout and venison to a choice of five different types of pie, prepared daily in "Ma's" kitchen and served family style in ample portions. Here too the Oregon Lumber Company spiked down their own rails into the timber and brought out logs to the big double-sided mill. Austin was an interesting and rugged town, with its string of saloons, stores with false fronts and a board sidewalk. The railroad facilities here included a wooden, four stall enginehouse, yard trackage and water tank.

In 1919 the new mill town of Batesville was established one mile west of Austin. Here the Oregon Lumber Company built a large white hotel at trackside with an adjacent dancehall that was the scene of many social events in that part of "cow country". It was from Batesville (the name was later shortened to Bates) that the Oregon Lumber Company built

The most classic structure on the Sumpter Valley Railway was the gently curving 60-foot high trestle at Alder Springs on the downgrade west of Larch. The location acquired its name from the abundance of Mountain Alder trees in the area, and became a popular picture stop in the early days. This venerable passenger train is handled by No. 5, newly renumbered from No. 1 in late 1906, but note the tender had not been repainted with the new number. Alder Springs was the scene of extensive logging operations at one time and the hillsides are still scarred with abandoned grades. — F. M. SHURT-LIFF This beautifully curving trestle served the railroad until the end as evidenced by the small view above of an 11-car train headed by Mallet No. 250 in 1941. — H. REID COLLECTION

The daily Sumpter Valley passenger train is met by stagecoach and touring car in this 1909 scene at Dixie, Oregon. Dixie station was located at the top of the grade out of Batesville. Switchbacks were used to get the line down to Prairie City. — HENRY R. GRIFFITHS COLLECTION

its long logging railroad down the John Day River. This line supplied logs to the new mill as long as the Sumpter Valley Railway operated.

On To Cattle Country

In 1908 valley folks around Prairie City were fearful that extension of the Oregon Lumber Company railroad down the Middle Fork of the John Day River would mean that they would be left off the railroad, which would continue via Galena and Monument, reach the main river at Kimberly, and continue on into Burns. They felt that interest in timber might outweigh the cattle and mining traffic potential of the main valley.

The Sumpter Valley's management had ambitious plans for the narrow gauge. They planned to build south, follow the John Day River past Blue Mountain Hot Springs and over the hump at Summit Prairie, then west across Logan Valley and finally down the Silvies River to Seneca and Burns. This final portion of the mileage to Burns would have been along the route of the present E. H. Hines Lumber Company's Oregon & Northwestern Railway.

An interesting story lies in the hope of the Sumpter Valley Railway to connect with the Nevada-California-Oregon Railroad, then being constructed out of Reno, Nevada. The Sumpter Valley could have obtained an easier grade and tapped more timber by taking over operations of the Oregon Lumber Company's logging railroad to Galena, but an optimistic management, still thinking of their line as a link in a large narrow gauge system, elected to build into Prairie City with expectations of eventually building on to John Day and a N-C-O connection. Had this dream of Eccles come true, it would have been possible for a traveler to go from the Owens Valley in southern California all the way to Baker City, Oregon, aboard narrow gauge coaches, except for the short ride from Mound House to Reno aboard the graceful standard gauge cars of the Virginia & Truckee Railroad. The route would have embraced the Carson & Colorado, Virginia & Truckee, Nevada-California-Oregon and Sumpter Valley. Though it never became a reality, the thought should excite the imagination of all narrow gauge historians.

An Extra Passenger

In 1911 logger Rube Kirkland's wife Delia was expecting, so she decided to go to Baker City to stay with relatives. Rube put his wife aboard the daily two-car passenger train at Tipton, and kissed his young wife goodbye. Shortly after the little Mogul pulled out of the Sumpter depot, Mrs. Kirkland went into labor. Resourceful conductor Dave Baird rushed all of the passengers out of the first coach and helped deliver a baby girl as the train barrelled through Salisbury as fast as the little 44-inch drivers could take it.

The Sumpter Valley's management, always looking for extra fares, were happy to set up special trains to carry folks along the line to the circus whenever it came to Baker City. Several special excursion cars were built for this service. There were also excursion trains for other special occasions, conventions, social gatherings and picnics. The Baker City Silver Cornet Band, under Professor Lewis E. Freitag, an employee of the Crystal Palace, was usually on hand for these specials. When Letson Balliet, general manager of the White Swan Mine, presented the band with new uniforms in 1901, the name was promptly changed to the White Swan Band. Still later the 15 piece ensemble was known as the Baker Mining Jubilee Band. It faded out of the picture along with the excursions on the narrow gauge.

In 1909 construction was begun on the final segment of the ambitious road. This extension running to Prairie City was 20 miles long and crossed the last of three summits at Dixie, highest point of the railroad. Dixie was exactly 5,280 feet above sea level and was reached by means of switchbacks and several hairpin curves. On Dixie Mountain it was necessary to either dig a tunnel or a deep cut. The builders decided to make the cut and work ceased just before Christmas. The road was completed into Prairie City the following year. The Sumpter Valley Railway was then 80 miles long.

Each fall cattle became a major source of rail traffic from Prairie City. Saturday evening about nine, a long stock train, usually double headed, left for Baker, where the cattle and sheep were put into stock pens for transfer to standard gauge cars for the haul to the Portland Union Stockyards, largest west of Kansas City or Omaha. The cattle would arrive there before dawn Monday, on a Union Pacific stock extra that originated at Pocatello and ran directly into the stockyards without interchange. The animals were quickly herded into pens to be ready for buyers who arrived at sunrise.

Prairie City traffic was good for a few years, with inbound shipments of feed and seed and equipment for local farmers and outbound farm products and cattle leaving aboard the tiny red cars. After World War I, though, traffic declined to the point that only a homemade motor car would make the run from Batesville to Prairie City, and eventually even that ceased.

Beginning Of The End

The beginning of the end came in January 1933, when the first mainline abandonment was authorized —from a point two miles south of Bates to Prairie (the City had since been dropped).

Formal passenger service came to its end at dusk on July 31, 1937, when engineer U. S. Carpenter brought the last varnish run into Baker from Bates. Carpenter had been in the cab of the train each trip since 1897. Fireman M. G. Hutchens was in the cab with Carpenter and allowed that he had fed 75,000 cords of wood into the firebox over the 20 years spent in the left hand seat. Completing the crew of the final train that hot summer evening were conductor William Larson, on the road since 1909, and 21-year veteran mail clerk Harold Marsh. Would-be passengers thereafter were accepted in the caboose, right up till the line was abandoned in 1947.

new cars will be transferred to other lines as fast as they can be replaced by cars of the remodeled type.

Home-Made Gasoline Motor Car for Auxiliary Service

The Sumpter Valley Railway, Baker, Ore., recently built in its shops a gasoline motor car for auxiliary service on its narrow-gage line. A 45-hp. White motor truck engine was used and the body was built to seat twenty-seven passengers. A light four-wheel pilot truck was set under the head end and a single pair of large diameter wheels to which power was transmitted served as the rear truck. The car was designed to make an average speed of 20 m.p.h. and operated over grades up to 4 per cent. Excellent service is reported for the thirty days during which the motor was in use. At the end of that time it was completely demolished in a head-on collision.

GASOLINE MOTOR CAR ON NARROW-GAGE ROAD OF SUMPTER VALLEY RAILWAY

Sumpter Valley's progressive management built this railcar for passenger service between Baker and Sumpter prior to World War I, but its service was limited to a month due to an unusual accident. — ELECTRIC RAILWAY JOURNAL

Sumpter Valley Railway's No. 11, that classic teakettle of 1878, was noted as being a fine steamer . . . mainly due to her copper firebox. At the right, the little Baldwin stands alongside the newly completed Tipton station in 1904 with a two car passenger train. F. M. Shurtliff was the hogger on that bright day, while N. W. Courtney handled the pine slabs. — F. M. SHURTLIFF In the view above, No. 11 when she was working for the Utah & Northern Railway at Logan, Utah, in 1885. The Mogul was presented to the University of Idaho after its Sumpter Valley service, but was donated to the scrap drive during the panic war year of 1942. — ARTHUR PETERSEN COLLECTION

Snow

The Endless Battle

Each winter presented an operating problem to the Sumpter Valley's management. With three summits in excess of 5,000 feet to cross, snow became an endless battle from late November through the spring thaws. The railway was unable to justify the purchase price for one of the new rotary or strange looking Jull snow plows. The battle against the white menace was fought with wedge plows, lines of little steamers coupled together and shovels manned by everyone from conductor to lumberjack. During the winter months, trains were delayed hours, days, and even longer on several occasions. The problem was complicated by the fact that all major sawmills, logging railroad lines and lumber camps were kept in operation throughout the winter. Since the logging operators had little or no snow removal equipment of their own, they were dependent on the Sumpter Valley's wedge plow in clearing the logging branches. Quite often a piece of geared motive power helped the Sumpter Valley's steamers push the old wedge. The Sumpter Valley was dependent on the logging traffic, for without this tonnage the mainline traffic would have trickled down to nothing.

In the scene above, the wedge plow in service at Tipton after a light snowfall. Snow alongside the track was already 15-feet deep when this photo was made. *(Right)* No. 2 with the daily passenger train after battling deep drifts on Rafferty Flat just east of Whitney. — BOTH MIKE WELTER COLLECTION

Effective snow fighting on the Sumpter Valley Railway was accomplished with the wedge snow plow. This plow shown on these two pages was built in the company shops at South Baker and saw many rebuildings over the years as a result of derailments, snowslides and the hazards associated with snow removal. In the scene above, the number one daily passenger train passes McEwen early in the morning with the wedge plow in front clearing off a light snowfall that fell during the night. The rising sun catches the train in silhouette as it dawns on a crisp clear morning . . . so clear that the engine's high-sounding whistle could be heard blowing for Lockhart ten miles away. — BROOKS HAWLEY (*Top-Opposite*) The wedge plow pictured at Austin in 1946. — HENRY R. GRIFFITHS

On a cold winter's morning engine No. 7 and her crew pause at Sumpter for photos shortly after the turn of the century. — ED HIBBS

Number Two Will Be A Few Days Late

In February 1916, a great storm hit eastern Oregon. The daily passenger train departed for the high country shortly after 8:00 A.M. and struggled into Austin only a little off schedule. Engine No. 17 with a load of empties coming up at a later time, became hopelessly wedged in high drifts on the four per cent grade below Larch. The passenger train heading home that afternoon with locomotive No. 1 got down to Johnson's Jumpoff where the freight train was stuck and after several attempts was unable to back up the steep grade. The snow continued to fall throughout the afternoon and evening as passengers huddled together in coach 21, while conductor David Baird did his best to keep the pot-bellied stove hot.

When the passenger train failed to reach Sumpter, a snow fighting train was hastily made up of all available motive power in the up-country. This rescue train consisted of a Sumpter Valley rod engine, W. H. Eccles Lumber Company's Heisler, Oregon Lumber Company's Heisler still lettered for her previous owner, Baker White Pine's Climax and the Sumper Valley's wedge plow. The train was one of the most unusual ever to operate on the line. The rescue outfit left Austin and proceeded slowly over the summit at Tipton, through Whitney and up the grade to Larch, encountering heavy drifts and ice clogged switches. The operation was slowed even more when the wedge plow jumped the track and had to be dug out before being rerailed.

Three days later the three car consist headed for Sumpter again, this time with seven engines plowing out the downgrade to the valley.

The winter of 1916 was a bad one for the Sumpter Valley. Pictured above is the rescue train headed for Sumpter with seven locomotives, two passenger cars and a caboose from the freight train that stalled on the four per cent grade. — MALLORY HOPE FERRELL COLLECTION

At the left, the grade at Tipton after it was finally cleared. — MIKE WELTER A Sumpter rod engine, W. H. Eccles Lumber Company Heisler, Oregon Lumber Company Heisler still lettered for the Nibley Lumber Company, and a Baker White Pine Climax head out of Austin with the rescue train. — CLAUDE GREEN COLLECTION

Passenger and crew of the stranded passenger train wait beside the deep drifts that trapped their train on the four per cent grade near Larch in 1916. — HENRY R. GRIFFITHS COLLECTION In the scene below, rescue efforts were slowed when the wedge plow jumped the tracks. — MALLORY HOPE FERRELL COLLECTION

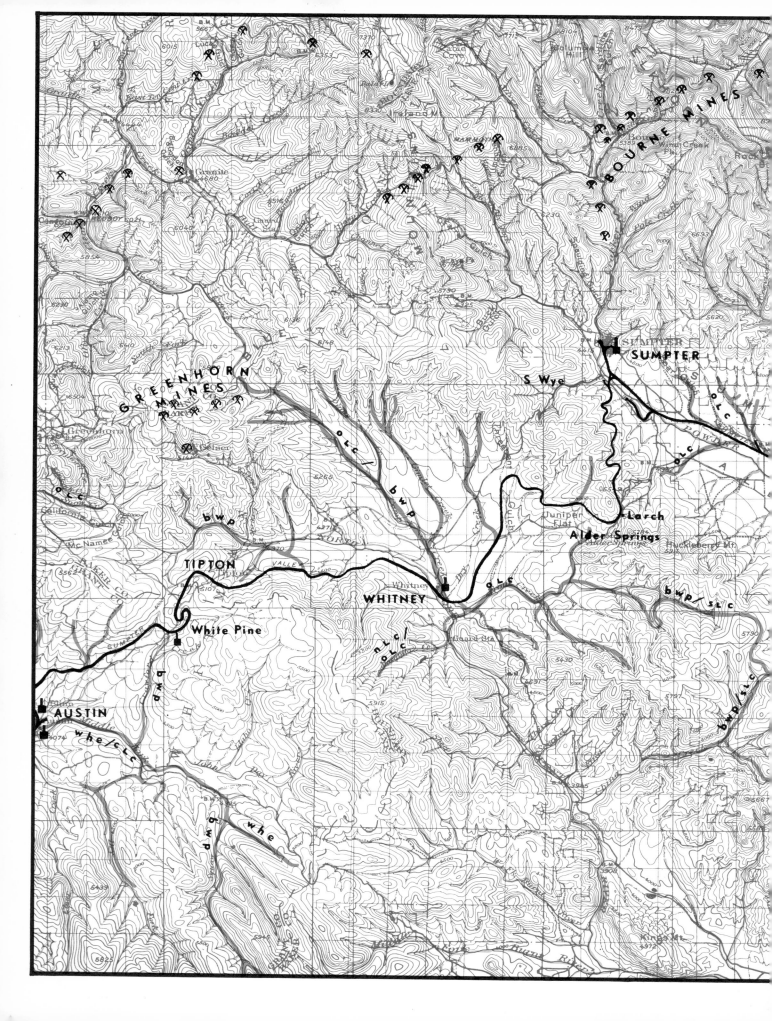

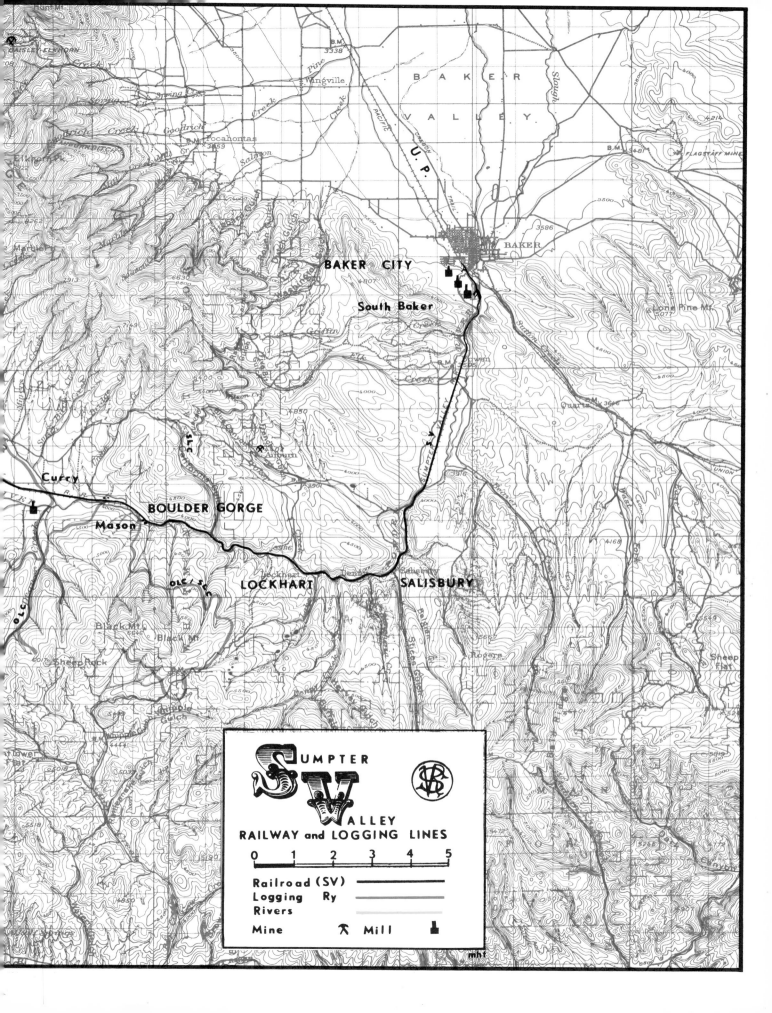

RAILWAY and LOGGING LINES

| 0 | 1 | 2 | 3 | 4 | 5 |

Railroad (SV) ────────
Logging   Ry ────────
Rivers   ────────

Mine ✕   Mill ◼

WRECKS

In 1911, the Oregon Railroad Commission cracked down on the Sumpter Valley for operating without a book of rules and dispatching trains without train orders. The result of such negligence resulted in several disastrous "cornfield meets". The commission demanded the Sumpter Valley Railway adopt the American Association of Railroads standard rules and operating procedures, then hire a superintendent who could enforce them. Edgar Burnham Pengra came to the scene from the Southern Pacific at Roseburg, Oregon, then part of the Harriman lines. Despite Ed Pengra's constant attempts to institute mainline operating rules, wrecks continued to occur on the twisting little narrow gauge. One salvation—they were seldom catastrophic.

Engines No. 10 and 14 staged this cornfield meet at Larch on September 18, 1913. — ED HIBBS-BROOKS HAWLEY COLLECTION

Consolidation type No. 10 upset her train near Dixie on March 12, 1915, when she hit some soft track near the switchback. — HENRY R. GRIFFITHS COLLECTION

Sumpter's homemade wrecker creaks and cables strain in its effort to right an overturned locomotive, while an Eccles Heisler smokes away in the background. — MIKE WELTER COLLECTION

In the scene above, engine No. 1 and the daily passenger train as it overturned at Alder Springs in 1927. — HENRY R. GRIFFITHS COLLECTION At the right, the results of a runaway train near Whitney when engineer Chris Karp lost the air on his mixed train. The train was traveling at such a speed when it left the rails, the cars completely cleared the main line. — MIKE WELTER COLLECTION

The Backshop Boys

The shops of the Sumpter Valley were located at South Baker, and it became a haven for wrecked, worn-out and broken equipment. The backshop boys could perform miracles with this ancient equipment. They constantly were overhauling, rebuilding, and overhauling the same pieces of equipment again.

They did such an excellent job the six connecting narrow gauge logging carriers favored the South Baker shops with their derelict cars. It was 1915 before the backshop boys saw their first new locomotive on the Sumpter. Over the years these men kept the trains running.

In the view above, machinists and blacksmiths gather for a wet plate photograph while the 1881 Brooks 2-6-0 they are rebuilding waits behind. (*Below*) Shop and train crews gather about No. 15 after an overhaul. (*Right*) The 1912 shop force waiting for another engine. (*Lower Right*) Tracy Miller working on one of the former Rio Grande 2-8-0's. — ALL WILLIAM A. ROUNDY COLLECTION

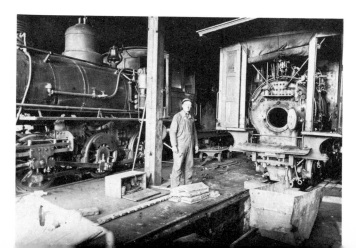

Posing on the Baker turntable are Knute Ferguson, Fred Metzler, J. D. White, D. L. Hiatt, J. W. Hansell, J. D. Jimmy, Bill Roundy, George A. Brunson and William Dunbreck with the trusty roundhouse dog. *(Center-Left)* Former Eureka-Nevada 2-8-0 given an overhaul by D. L. Hiatt and Bill Roundy in 1912. *(Center-Right)* Boiler washing report for engine No. 16. *(Lower)* Famous western railroad photographer Fred Jukes photographed the shop crew gathered about newly repainted Tonopah Ry. No. 4 in 1907. — ALL WILLIAM A. ROUNDY COLLECTION

Form 400—6-23-25—1M RB34733

Sumpter Valley Railway Company

BOILER WASHING REPORT

Engine No. *16* of the SUMPTER VALLEY RAILWAY COMPANY

Had boiler washed *Sept 28* 1928 at *Baker*

By *Anton Walters* Were all washout plugs removed? *Yes*

Were gauge cock and water glass spindles removed and cleaned? *Yes*

By whom? *H. A. Finlayson*

J. H. Carpenter,
Foreman in charge.

Prairie City and Beyond . . .

Thinking of itself as more than a narrow gauge short line, the Sumpter Valley Railway in 1909 began what was to be the final segment of this ambitious little road. The Prairie City extension was to be 20 miles in length, and would reach the highest point on the railroad. At 5,280 feet above sea level, Dixie became the last of three major summits. This last summit was overcome by means of hairpin curves and switchbacks.

Prairie City was not a lumber or mining town. Here cattle provided the major source of revenue for the new line. During stock season long cattle trains, usually double-headed, left Prairie City every Saturday night in order to make connections with the Union Pacific's stock extra into the huge Portland Union Stockyards. It was contemplated the Sumpter Valley might make a connection with the then a-building Nevada-California-Oregon Railway out of Reno, Nevada. Cattle traffic never reached the potential, and the Prairie City extension was the first portion of the mainline abandoned when tracks were removed in 1933.

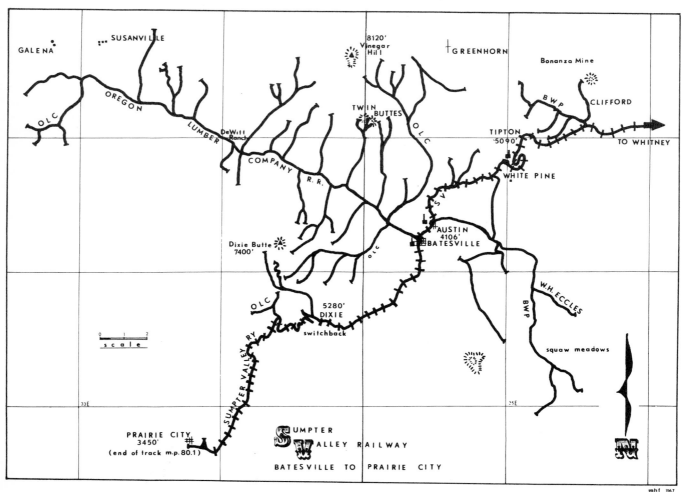

mhf 1967

The engineer with oilcan in hand mounts his iron horse as passengers and mail are transferred to a waiting stagecoach at Prairie City depot in 1915. — ARTHUR PETERSEN COLLECTION (Left) This gay crowd of passengers prepares to leave Prairie City aboard the little green coaches of the Sumpter Valley's daily passenger train. — MIKE WELTER COLLECTION (Below) In 1910 the Sumpter Valley aspired to connect with the narrow gauge Nevada-California-Oregon Railway then building northward from Reno, Nevada. In this scene, No. 5 a handsome 4-6-0 switches at Reno shortly after its arrival from the Baldwin Locomotive Works in far off Philadelphia. — STANLEY G. PALMER

Sawdust In The Air

THE MOTIVATING force behind the Sumpter Valley Railway was the cry Timber-r-r-r! The humming saws of the mills were hungry for logs, digesting them as fast as the little teakettles could haul them from hillside to millpond.

Oregon Lumber Company

For its productive lifetime, the Sumpter Valley Railway would be known as an integral part of the expanding Oregon Lumber Company complex, which was to eventually include the standard gauge Mount Hood Railroad, other mills at Dee, Oregon, and lumber interests throughout the west.

Organized in 1889 by David Eccles, the firm built a small mill just south of Baker City that year. Eccles' partners in the venture were C. W. Nibley and John Stoddard, whose names were soon to appear on the mastheads of their own lumber enterprises.

Almost immediately the lumber company became involved in promoting a railroad to tap the thriving mining and lumber areas to the west. Oregon Lumber Company supplied the capital for the construction of the Sumpter Valley Railway and received its first carload of logs from what later became Dean Siding on August 1, 1891, less than a year after the road was chartered.

As the rails of the Sumpter Valley Railway were pushed up the Powder River valley, timber was taken from each gulch and creek along the way. In 1893, a planing mill was built beside the South Baker sawmill, for the production of molding, lathe and finished lumber.

ꝏꝏꝏ

Lumbering district of Baker with Oregon Lumber Co.'s mill and Baker White Pine in the distance against a background of untouched forest at Whitney Flat before the sawers came. — **BROOKS HAWLEY AND CLAUDE GREEN**

Until this time, the motive power operated by the Sumpter Valley was sufficient for both mainline and logging activities, as most of the cutting was relatively close to the common carrier's trackage. In 1898 the Oregon Lumber Company purchased the first of many geared locomotives, having observed the success of the Shay designed engine purchased earlier that year by the Stoddard Brothers for their logging operation.

Grass hardly had a chance to grow between the pine ties at Sumpter when the Oregon Lumber Company pushed its yard-wide tracks in search of timber from S Wye towards Larch, the first of three summits. The lumber company systematically pushed on into new timber and the common carrier brought cash into the company tills by hauling out the logs of its parent and other lumber firms. Soon after new tracks were spiked down, passenger service was inaugurated to bring in the lumberjacks and their supplies. This was a time when towns sprang up overnight and became ghost towns as fast as tall trees became short stumps.

As logging spurs were put down in ever increasing numbers, the need arose for more specialized motive power, and the Oregon Lumber Company acquired a fleet of narrow gauge Shays, later to be supplemented by a stable of Heislers, a lone Climax and an unwanted Sumpter Valley 4-4-0. This stepchild had once seen service out of Mound House, Nevada, on the old Carson & Colorado Railway.

The *Timberman*, a journal of northwestern logging news, reported in the spring of 1903 that the Oregon Lumber Company was using the only steam skidder in the state. This machine was used to daylight the forest around Whitney. It was a converted Lima built steam shovel, very much like the later Decker patent loader, on which the flat cars passed through the machine. The loader was used by Bill Scott's crew until about 1909, when it was discarded because of its huge size, heavy weight and slow speed.

Soon after the 36-inch gauge tracks reached Austin in the autumn of 1905, work was begun on a new

sawmill. This mill operated in the decade preceding 1919, when a new mill and town were constructed one mile away at Batesville.

Batesville was complete with company houses, hotel, store and dancehall. Named after an Eccles family friend, Paul C. Bates, the name was later shortened to the more formal form of Bates, and continued to supply lumber even after the Sumpter Valley Railway and the Oregon Lumber Company ceased operations. Bates was also the point from which the logging railroads of the Oregon Lumber Company radiated into the tall timber. Most notable of these lines was the 20 mile road down the middle fork of the John Day River, with its more than 40 miles of branches.

In 1915, when the new Nibley Lumber Company mill at Whitney burned, Oregon Lumber Company finished cutting Nibley's timber and obtained their big Heisler locomotive. In 1928, Oregon Lumber Company rebuilt the Nibley mill, but did not operate it until 1932, because of the Depression. This mill continued in operation until all the good timber in the area was gone and was finally junked in the mid-thirties.

When railroad logging operations out of Bates ended during World War II, Shay No. 7 was used for a brief period in switching service at Baker and finally to tear up the mainline in 1947, thus bringing to an end almost 60 years of narrow gauge logging operations for the company.

Little two-truck Shay No. 102 of the Oregon Lumber Company loads logs at Trout Creek on October 7, 1915. This view clearly shows the loading of logs using a gypsy engine. A gypsy was a combination locie and donkey with two horizontal spools mounted on the engine where the pilot should be. The spools were powered by a crankshaft which could be thrown into operation by a clutch. It must have been a sight to see this Shay yarding logs with the hogger acting as donkey puncher. Left to right: Bill Johnson the camp boss, Cleve Nolan, Jess Smith, Frank Corn and Claude Green, long time logging engineer who worked on Shay, Climax and Heisler geared engines.

— CLAUDE GREEN COLLECTION

Oregon Lumber Company's Heisler No. 104 switches at Bates, Oregon, during the pre-war calm of July 1940. — EMERY J. ROBERTS At the left, Climax No. 105 built for New Mexico's Halleck & Howard Lumber Co. in 1919 is shown on the Sumpter Valley's main line near Baker after being rebuilt in the railroad shops. — EARL EMLAW

Snow seldom prevented loggers of Sumpter Valley country from hauling out the timber on schedule. In this scene, Oregon Lumber Company's Heisler No. 104 and Shay No. 102 were photographed bucking deep snow on Tipton Mountain above Whitney in 1932.
— HENRY R. GRIFFITHS FROM CLAUDE GREEN COLLECTION

Plowing out spur logging tracks was often an undertaking. During February 1916, Oregon Lumber Company's Heisler and a Climax from Baker White Pine shove aside the white menace. — CLAUDE GREEN

53

Oregon Lumber Company 4th of July employee excursion near Whitney in 1915. Train is drawn by No. 103, a 4-4-0 from Eureka & Palisade. — CLAUDE GREEN

A Wayward Eight-wheeler

In the summer of 1915, the Oregon Lumber Company had a logging camp at the mouth of Trout Creek, near McCoy siding, three miles from Whitney. The former Carson & Colorado 4-4-0 was used to pull a short link-n-pin flatcar to haul supplies from Whitney to the camp. The flatcar once had been used as a Sumpter Valley Railway excursion car, and occasionally was used on outings and picnic specials for lumber company employees and their families.

One day Bill Scott, the camp boss, and his iron burner pulled up and began loading freight aboard the flat at Whitney when little No. 103 began to move. Off rolled the 4-4-0, gaining distance on her pursuing crew with each puff of steam. The engine ran through an open stub switch, left the rails and bounced along the ties, and then hit a split switch which put the old girl back on the rails again! Off she went down the Sumpter Valley Railway mainline, picking up speed as she clicked off the miles.

Further ahead, a mystified Claude Green, veteran logging engineer, was puzzled as to why the approaching No. 103 wasn't blowing for the crossings, and why as the locomotive drew nearer no-one waved from the cab. Making a flying leap for the gangway as she passed, the intrepid Green pulled himself into the cab and brought the wanderer to a halt before staging a "cornfield meet" with an unsuspecting passenger train, then on its way.

Cause of the incident, a leaking throttle. When the No. 103 pulled up the crew failed to set the brakes. When the steam from the leaking throttle had built up enough pressure to start the engine, the old girl began to move. Without the brakes applied, there was nothing to hold her.

Early post card scene circa 1913 lettered "Slow Train of Logs near Whitney." It shows Oregon Lumber Shay No. 102 at the left and 4-4-0 No. 10. — MALLORY HOPE FERRELL COLLECTION

In 1905 the Oregon Lumber Company used four of these high wheel carts to haul logs to the railhead. — CLAUDE GREEN COLLECTION

Oregon Lumber Company crews crosshaul a log in this scene. This was done by passing a line over and under, then pulling on it to roll the log up a set of incline skids. Horses out of sight provide the power. — CLAUDE GREEN

In 1904 the Oregon Lumber Company converted a Lima steam shovel into a log loader. The empty cars ran through the machine on a section of inclined rail. This loader was finally discarded in 1909 on account of its being too heavy, wide and slow. — CLAUDE GREEN COLLECTION

BAKER WHITE PINE LUMBER CO.

Frank Gardinier's Baker White Pine Lumber Company started in 1912, and the company's first mill was built beside the Sumpter Valley Railway at White Pine. Baker White Pine immediately built three-foot gauge logging railroads into their timber holdings and ordered a brand new Climax locomotive from the Corry, Pennsylvania, builder. The success of this engine was such that in 1913 a second and slightly heavier Climax was ordered, followed two years later by still another. A mill was later constructed in Baker, and it was for a time one of the largest mills in Oregon.

The geared motive power hauled out the logs to sidings on the Sumpter Valley Railway and each night during the heyday of logging, the Sumpter Valley would deliver the cars to the big White Pine millpond. World War I demand for airplane spruce was such that the Sumpter Valley could not keep ahead of the need for logs in the three major mills at Baker. These were the days of big timber too!

Each afternoon and evening the common carrier would work at getting 70-90 cars of logs down to Sumpter, enough to make up two full trains of logs for the Oregon Lumber Company, Stoddard Lumber Company, and the White Pine's hungry saws.

Baker White Pine was one outfit that would not suspend its logging because of snow. Its camps operated all year long, and there were few times when the snow got too deep for Gardinier's boys. When the snow got too deep for horses, the steam skidders pulled the logs across the ice and snow. One old timer proudly said he "brought in log trains when the thermometer was two feet below zero," and he produced a picture to prove his point!

The White Pine outfit had their own log cars—even used a former Sumpter Valley side door caboose on their log trains. Bad wrecks were rare on the White Pine's trackage. William Baker, the long time logging superintendent, built his logging railroads to mainline standards, a factor which contributed to the failure of the firm in 1929, when its holdings were taken over by the Stoddard Brothers.

While it ran, Baker White Pine Lumber Company was a first class operation.

The Climax design became the most popular power on Baker White Pine Lumber Company's railroad operation. Over the years Frank Gardinier purchased three of the Corry-built machines for service on his road. At the left, artist Casey Holtzinger depicts a scene of White Pine's No. 1 blasting through a stump forest above Dale Creek in 1911.

Baker White Pine logged their timber holdings summer and winter. Climax No. 2 is seen loading logs during the winter of 1915. Note the deer antlers affixed to the oil headlight and the gypsy-rigged loader.
— BRUCE MOREHEAD

Logging In Pine Country

The first logging in Sumpter Valley utilized four-legged motive power. Next wooden rails were laid and horses pulled the logs to the mill on small wide-flanged cars. With the arrival of steam motive power, horses, mules, and oxen were still used to load the logs and skid them to the loading docks. In 1903 the Oregon Lumber Company used a steam skidder and loader on their Dean Creek Line, the first in the northwest. This machine was adapted from a Lima steam shovel and saw several years service before being discarded in 1909 as too large, heavy, and slow.

Perhaps the most popular innovation in logging in the pine country was the introduction of small (6x7 inch cylinders) Lidgerwood steam gypsy loading engines, which were bolted to the pilot beam and powered by steam from the locomotive's boiler. These loaders proved very successful and saw service for as long as logs continued to roll into the mills

Casey Holtzinger's drawing at the right depicts one of the Baker White Pine's American Hoist & Derrick steam skidders at work on Camp Creek above Whitney. (*Below*) Climax No. 3 of Baker White Pine stands by as a slide-back loader draws logs aboard the privately owned flats near Tipton in 1922. This crew could load 136,000 board feet per day summer and winter. Note the extra high stack of wood slabs in the tender. — CLAUDE GREEN COLLECTION

aboard narrow gauge cars. In connection with the gypsy engines, the loggers also used the Hansen Jammer. This jammer consisted of an A-frame on a sled, which could be pulled back over the cars, loading the car in front of it as it moved along. Another variation was the A-frame mounted at the trackside loading dock, a technique which was used by Oregon Lumber Company and Eccles Lumber Co.

Slide-back loaders were employed on many of the narrow gauge logging railroads and were popular on the Baker White Pine Lumber Company's trackage. The White Pine likewise used small American steam skidders in their operations. These steam skidders proved more powerful and faster than the small locomotive-mounted Lidgerwoods. This enabled one crew to load up to 136,000 board feet per day. These loaders were moved back atop the line of flatcars, loading the adjacent car as it went back. The term "Slide-Back" loader came to be applied to all loaders operated in this manner.

W. H. Eccles Lumber Company uses an A-frame loader and the gypsy engine mounted on the pilot beam of Climax No. 1 to load logs near Austin in 1911. — B. H. WARD COLLECTION

A new steam skidder arrives in the woods and is unloaded by a Baker White Pine crew. — CLAUDE GREEN COLLECTION

TWO FEET BELOW ZERO
Logging In The Snow On The Baker White Pine Lumber Company

The Baker White Pine Lumber Company was one outfit that operated all-year long. Camps were open no matter how deep the snow and there were few days when Frank Gardinier's boys did not roll in the log trains. In the scene above and below, an American slide-back loader may be seen loading logs in deep snow with former Sumpter Valley Railway caboose, Climax No. 3 and Baker White Pine log cars. — BOTH CLAUDE GREEN COLLECTION

Climax No. 3 with a gypsy-rigged loader on its pilot moves a skidder to a new location in 1915. — BRUCE MOOREHEAD At the right, China Creek Camp rests in the deep snow of 1923. — CLAUDE GREEN In the scene below, camp cars repose in deep snow during White Pine's youthful years. Camp cars were the loggers' home on wheels which served as quarters, chow house and storage. — CLAUDE GREEN COLLECTION

Under a rolling cloud of woodsmoke, Climax No. 2 of the Baker White Pine Lumber Company smokes its way across a low timber trestle while bringing out a load of logs to the Sumpter Valley main line connection. — BRUCE MOREHEAD

Steel rails across canyons on wood bridges that stood 60 to 75 feet above the valley floor were the best substitute for solid ground. The huge Curry line trestle was an engineering feat for Sumpter Valley country, and provided thrills for those rail loggers who rode the geared engines and shaking log cars across the gorge. — BROOKS HAWLEY

The early construction train of the Baker White Pine provided transportation to the woods for the dapper young men aboard the tank and the lady in the cab of Climax No. 2. Oil headlights and link 'n pin couplers date this scene as circa 1913. — BRUCE MOREHEAD

Logging trains by virtue of light rail, hastily built track, steep grades and heavy loads were often plagued by derailments, runaways and the like. The remains of a Baker White Pine runaway on the Curry Branch in 1923 lie at the bottom of a fill in the scene above, and cars scattered all along the grade as evidenced at the left. — CLAUDE GREEN

Whoops!

Logging wrecks rarely killed the crews, since they usually "joined the birds" (jump off in great haste from any moving equipment in danger of accident) or cut the train loose when they started to runaway. In these scenes a minor derailment caused by a broken axle on Climax No. 1. Note the A-frame Hansen Jammer on the flatcar at the left. — BOTH WARREN K. MILLER COLLECTION

Stoddard Brothers second engine, *Old Brigham*, brings out loads from California Gulch in 1904 — WILLIAM A. ROUNDY

"Old Brigham", and in 1917 purchased a new 36-ton Heisler.

The Stoddard loggers equipped their engines with the locally popular Lidgerwood gypsy engines, which were mounted on the pilot beam and used for loading logs. Train crews did most of the actual log loading on Stoddard operations, and the same practice was found on the other logging railroads of the area. In 1922 another new Heisler was purchased and the two original iron horses were set out to pasture.

STODDARD LUMBER CO.

Stoddard Brothers entered the lumber business in 1892, shortly after the narrow gauge reached McEwen. George and Joseph first erected a small sawmill on Clear Creek. Shortly thereafter they used a horse-powered pole road to transport logs down to their mill.

In 1897 the Sumpter Valley Railway purchased a secondhand, two-cylinder Shay from an Arkansas logger for the Stoddard Brothers Lumber Company. This engine was called "Old Betsy", and served the Stoddards for many years.

Logging operations quickly expanded and a new mill was built in South Baker near the Oregon Lumber Company's thriving plant. The company continued to operate with one locomotive, however. In the summer of 1902, while bringing out several cars of logs to the Sumpter Valley mainline, one log bogie jumped the track on a trestle, pulling the locomotive and two other cars with it. While no one was hurt, the sole locomotive was badly damaged and put out of service until the South Baker shops could repair it. This incident emphasized the need for another engine on the six-mile road.

The year 1903 saw the arrival of the Stoddards' second engine, this one a 25-ton Heisler purchased from a West Virginia logger. Like her predecessor this one was known not by a number, but by the name of "Old Brigham". She was put to work bringing logs out of California Gulch, but had a lifetime plagued with runaways, wrecks, and derailments. On her very first job she tipped over and killed engineer Bob Duvall.

Stoddard Brothers Lumber Company became Stoddard Lumber Company in 1914 when they bought out the Shockley & McMurran Lumber Company. They continued to haul logs with "Old Betsy" and

When the Stoddards assumed control of the Baker White Pine properties in 1929, they gained three Climax locomotives. To avoid a conflict in numbering, the former No. 3 Stoddard Heisler became the No. 5.

Stoddard continued narrow gauge logging operations on its private trackage and extended the former Baker White Pine lines to the headwaters of China Creek and other new virgin timber areas.

Stoddard log trains operated into Baker until 1943. However, nearby Stoddard's Heisler powered standard gauge, common carrier, called the Big Creek & Telocaset Railroad, continued to run for a few more years after the Baker operation shut down.

Stoddard Lumber Co. Heisler No. 4 brings a train of logs into Baker. This 40-ton engine was built new for Stoddard in 1922. — COLLECTION OF VERNON GOE & JOHN LABBE

Stoddard's *Old Brigham* was noted for running away, tipping over and killing her engineers. On her very first run she killed engineer Bob Duvall. In the scene above, old No. 4 is photographed moving two flats of rail and a carload of hay at Johnson's Jumpoff, just below Larch. — CLAUDE GREEN COLLECTION Below, No. 4 loads logs near Baker in the twilight of her career in July 1941. — AL FARROW

W. H. ECCLES LUMBER CO.

In 1910 the Sumpter Valley Railway and its owner, Oregon Lumber Company, fell into disfavor with the U. S . Forest Service over disputed timberlands. The result of this head-on collision between the company and the government caused the formation of several independent but closely related lumber firms in order to obtain Forest Service timber.

It was, therefore, no surprise to find Bill Eccles, brother of David Eccles, setting up his W. H. Eccles Lumber Company in 1911. The new firm secured a large tract of government timber in the Blue Mountains and started production of interior finish, sash, door, molding, and siding from the white pine on the hillsides around Austin. The Wisconsin-Oregon Lumber Company's Baker City mill was purchased and moved to Austin. To get logs to his new 75,000 board foot band mill, a brand new narrow gauge Climax locomotive was ordered. This engine arrived in September 1911, just in time to start hauling logs into the mill aboard five new log cars built from parts ordered from the Railway Equipment Company. The following year saw three and one-half miles of logging spurs in operation under H. H. Salisbury, the dynamic logging supervisor. After observing the Heisler geared locomotives on neighboring trackage of the Oregon Lumber Company, Stoddard Lumber Company and Nibley Lumber Company, the Eccles outfit ordered a two-truck Heisler and the following year received another Heisler, which had been returned to the plant by the original owner.

The W. H. Eccles engines continued to haul logs to the Austin millpond until the government tract was largely depleted. In 1922 Climax No. 1 was shipped to a new Eccles operation at Cascade, Idaho, where it was used for several years. Then Cavanaugh Lumber Company brought the 32-ton Climax back from Cascade to Sumpter Valley country for their new operation in 1929. Heisler No. 2 had already been sold to the Oregon Lumber Company and Heisler No. 3 was sold to the Halleck & Howard Lumber Company at Cascade. In 1926 the W. H. Eccles Lumber Company faded from the Sumpter Valley scene for good.

Eccles Lumber Company loggers combine know-how, strong cables, mule power and donkey power from the gypsy engine on Heisler No. 3 to load this nice piece of pine aboard an awaiting log car. These operations at Austin in 1917 are being observed from the locomotive gangway by future jacks. Old Heisler No. 3 is very much alive today although not running. It was discovered resting in a shed at Cascade, Idaho. — BERT WARD COLLECTION

W. H. Eccles Lumber Company's Heisler No. 3 steams patiently during the winter of 1917 while her crew pose for a snapshot. Left to right: Earl Moran, Claude Green, Clarence Vandervort and camp boss Holton. — CLAUDE GREEN COLLECTION

The Eccles mill was moved from Baker City to the meadow just above Austin in 1911. Eccles Lumber had a finishing mill, yard and office in Baker City. In the view below, Climax No. 1 dumps logs into the Austin mill pond. The engine was painted W. S. Eccles instead of W. H. Eccles at the factory and the situation was not rectified until the next painting. — BOTH BERT WARD COLLECTION

Nibley Lumber Company's Heisler No. 2 was built as a standard gauge machine in 1910 and saw service on the Blue Mountain Railroad before being cut down to 3-foot gauge in the Sumpter Valley shops. The engine later became Oregon Lumber Co. No. 104. — JIM GERTZ COLLECTION

THE SMALL LOGGERS

Nibley Lumber Company

C. W. Nibley, president of the Oregon Lumber Company when the Sumpter Valley Railway began, was a trusted friend of David Eccles. In 1910 when the Oregon Lumber Company fell into disfavor with the U. S. Forest Service over some timber deals in the Whitney area, the Nibley Hilgard Lumber Company mill was moved to Whitney. Nibley brought a standard gauge Heisler with him from his Blue Mountain Railroad and the Baker shops cut the engine down to three-foot gauge. They sent her over the hill to Whitney, where she was used to build a logging railroad down the North Fork of the Burnt River in 1913.

In 1915 the Nibley mill burned and the Heisler and other properties were taken over by the Oregon Lumber Company. The Oregon Lumber Company rebuilt the Nibley mill in 1928 and it operated from 1932 until all the good timber was gone, and the mill was junked.

The former standard gauge Heisler continued to run under the Oregon Lumber Company herald for many years. She was top heavy, but a powerful engine and the favorite for snow plowing duties.

Cavanaugh Lumber Company

Cavanaugh Lumber Company was built by Frank Gardinier in 1929, after the failure of his Baker White Pine Lumber Company. A secondhand Climax was purchased from W. H. Eccles and shipped back to the Sumpter Valley country from Cascade, Idaho.

Construction was begun on a new mill on Bridge Creek near Bates and the Climax was used to build the mill, yard and woods tracks. Before the mill was completed, the Depression caught up with another logger, and the order came through to halt all construction. The Oregon Lumber Company then hauled Cavanaugh's timber to its Bates Mill and the Cavanaugh Lumber Company ceased even before the first saw cut was made.

Sumpter's Last Stand

ARRIVAL in 1915 of the first 2-8-2 locomotives from the Baldwin Locomotive Works was quite an event at South Baker. No. 16 and her two sisters were the first new engines the little road ever owned, and they provided the mainstay of motive power for the next 25 years. At this same time the car shops began rebuilding much of the old worn out rolling stock, using parts from the original secondhand equipment of the early 1890's.

Four new pieces of passenger equipment began arriving in 1918 from the St. Charles carbuilders. These salmon colored cars graced the daily passenger trains for the next two decades, and after retirement some of them went on to see additional service on the White Pass & Yukon line in Alaska.

With the removal of the Bates to Prairie City line in 1933 and the end of all passenger service four years later, the Sumpter Valley Railway forsook David Eccles' hope that his line would become part of a narrow gauge system. Again, lumber became the only commodity of note to grace the ledgers of the slim gauge line.

When Colorado's gilsonite-hauling Uintah Railway narrow gauge closed down in 1939, Sumpter Valley management purchased the defunct line's remarkable pair of Lucien Sprague designed Mallets. These articulated machines were the largest ever built for an American narrow gauge railroad. South Baker shops promptly converted them to oil burners, removed their side tanks and fitted them with regular tenders, thus drastically improving their esthetic appearance in the process.

The two Mallets provided some of the finest steam action in the northwest during and following the war years. Powerful as they were, the baby 2-6-6-2's were still required to double the four per cent grade out of S Wye to Larch. Their braking capacity was sufficient to let down the loaded lumber trains at an easy 15 miles per hour. Earlier power, by contrast, had been limited by their inability to provide air for braking loads, and runaways in the days of small locomotives were not uncommon.

With the decline of freight traffic following World War II, the Mallets provided sufficient power to handle the needs of the Sumpter Valley. Gradually, the company sold off all its small locomotives, some for scrap, others for continued use in Peru and Alaska.

The handwriting that portended abandonment appeared in the crew assignments scribbled on the office call board at South Baker, as weekly round trips were reduced to three in 1946. No longer did logging trains puff anywhere near the valley, and the tri-weekly freight had the road all to itself, with a Mallet thundering on the head end, and trailing were cars of fresh smelling lumber. At the tail end of the train, a tiny bobber in which right up till the very end, an occasional paying passenger might find accommodation.

A bright summer day in 1947 marked the final steam mainline run over the Sumpter Valley Railway. For all practical purposes, when engineer Chris Karp wheeled No. 251 and its train into South Baker that day, the real Sumpter Valley Railway ceased to exist.

It is true that at Baker a dual gauge remnant of the road, diesel powered and a couple of miles long, continued to operate under Oregon Lumber Company and later Edward Hines Lumber Company ownership. But even this shadow of the once great Sumpter Valley went out of existence on December 27, 1961, with the abandonment of the last 1.5 miles of switching trackage, along with the former Oregon Lumber Company mill.

Here then was the last stand of the Sumpter Valley Railway. . .

Steaming winter action with Sumpter Valley's No. 251 near Boulder Gorge on December 30, 1946. A leaking steam pipe and five degree temperature below zero produced this thundering effect beside the bubbling Powder River. — RICHARD KINDIG

Lucius Beebe FOCUSES ON THE SUMPTER VALLEY

The late bon vivant of railroading, Lucius Beebe, photographed the Sumpter Valley Railway in the mid-forties. With his partner Charles Clegg, he captured on film some of the finest action scenes on the line which he held in deep affection. In a letter shortly before his death, Beebe wrote, "I shall never forget the wonderment and splendor of the railroad in the bright noontide of its going. The Polygamy Central was something to behold and I trust these graphics portray it as you desire."

In the scene above, 2-8-2 No. 16, first new locomotive ever owned by the Sumpter eases 25 cars westbound near Sumpter in 1939. At the right, the same train is photographed blasting out of Baker yards. Second car on the train was used to haul sawdust from the Bates mill. BOTH HENRY R. GRIFFITHS *(Left)* Photographed in the World War I era was brand new No. 17 with a loaded lumber train headed for Baker City. *(Top-Opposite)* The same engine receives assistance in moving a mixed drag over the Tipton grade. — BOTH FRED JUKES

WOODBURNING MIKES

Sumpter Valley's woodburning Mikes were numbered 16 through 20, and were among the few new loco-motives owned by the slim gauge. Purchased between 1915 and 1920, the first three came from Baldwin and the last two from American. These woodburners saw constant service until the Uintah Mallets ar-rived. Before long the 2-8-2 Mikados were no longer needed, the Baldwins being sold to the Peruvian Government, while the American products were shippped north to Alaska for service on the White Pass & Yukon Route.

SMOKE
IN THE GORGE

Located 16 miles west of Baker City, Boulder Gorge was perhaps the most beautiful spot on the entire railroad. Early photographers were quick to capture this scene on their postcards. The railroad crossing of the Powder River at the bottom of the gorge was known as Red Bridge due to its early boxcar red color. Later this bridge was rebuilt as a trestle, but it still was Red Bridge. The views on these pages were made from essentially the same place on the old stage road to Sumpter. Above, Red Bridge in the mid 1890's. — MALLORY HOPE FERRELL COLLECTION At the right, photographer Henry R. Griffiths portrays 2-8-2 No. 16 with a westbound train in the calm prior to World War II. *(Below)* In the early days, the stage road was so narrow as to permit one wagon or the new horseless carriage over the road at a time. Someone had to back up if two vehicles met on the ever twisting highway. This scene is from an old postcard circa 1923. — BROOKS HAWLEY COLLECTION

The flats around Sumpter and the river below were toiled first by white miners with pan 'n sluice box, then by the Chinese brought west by railroads. After hardrock mining had essentially ceased, the ground around Sumpter down Cracker Creek and along the Powder River was reworked by floating dredges.

The original dredge chewed up the ground immediately above Sumpter in the early 1900's. In 1935 the Sumpter Valley Dredging Company launched a huge "Yuba" type dredge which operated both day and night until World War II put an end to gold mining. The war also took with it a number of struggling narrow gauge railroads throughout the West.

Shortly after the war, the Powder River Dredging Co. reactivated the bucket line machine and it dug its way south to its final resting place below Sumpter in 1954. Gold bearing soil was found beneath the Sumpter Valley Railway's tracks at S Wye and the line relocated into the tailings so that gold might be digested by the dredge.

Today the 1,200-ton monster rests at the site of its final diggings. The riffled piles of rocks are reminders of an era when gold was found on the Sumpter Valley right-of-way.

The top view shows gold dredge Number One that worked near S Wye between 1913-1924. — MIKE WELTER The huge "Yuba" dredge is shown in the center. — WALT MENDENHALL At the right, Sumpter's Mallet on the relocated right-of-way. — HENRY R. GRIFFITHS Below, the tracks at S Wye relocated into the tailings. — AL FARROW

ROUNDUP
ON THE
NARROW GAUGE

In 1915 a Sumpter Valley train stopped at S Wye to change the switch and then head for Baker City with her string of 18 loaded cattle cars. Trackage was on a sharp curve with a four per cent downgrade. As the engineer released the brakes, the entire train flipped over on its side. The locomotive stayed on the track, but all four-legged passengers took to the hills when the roofs of the former Union Pacific cars popped off. Several factors contributed to the mishap. Some brakes did not release and nearly all the cattle shifted their weight to the inside of the slightly elevated trackage at about the same time. A slight tug on the drawbar was all that was needed to put the whole show on the ground. This escapade started the biggest railroader roundup in Sumpter Valley history. None of the cattle were killed, but the stock cars were a complete loss. — BROOKS HAWLEY COLLECTION

Stump Dodger cattlemen were upset with the small Class XM stockcars the Sumpter used to carry stock in during the rush season. They raised such an uproar at their prize stock being shipped with bowed heads that management sent the cars to the Baker Shops to have caboose-like cupolas installed on the 27-footers. The new feature allowed livestock to assume their normal posture while traveling. At the right, one of the rebuilt cars involved in a wreck near Larch Summit on Sept. 18, 1913. — WILLIAM ROUNDY COLLECTION

COMING

THE UINTAH MALLETS WERE IMPRESSIVE

The narrow gauge Uintah Railway, located along the Colorado-Utah boundary was blessed with seven and one-half per cent grades, 80 degree curves and operating altitude of 8,437 feet at Baxter Pass . . . unusual conditions in any railroad man's book. General manager Lucien C. Sprague, later to win fame as the genius of the Minneapolis & St. Louis Railway's rehabilitation, designed and Baldwin built the first of two articulated 2-6-6-2T engines in 1926. The curves were widened to a formidable 66 degrees to accommodate the slim gauge monsters. In 1939 the Uintah Railway abandoned its twisting trackage. The baby Mallets were loaded on flatcars at Mack, Colorado, and sent to the

or GOING...

big sky country of Sumpter Valley.

Shortly after arriving on the Polygamy Central in June 1940, the engines were renumbered Nos. 250 and 251. They had their side tanks removed and received tenders from Alaska-bound Mikados. Fuel was changed from coal to oil. In a true sense of the word the engines were not Mallets at all but four cylinder simple locomotives. They were widely known as Mallets and the name stuck despite the purist. The two engines were the largest built for any narrow gauge duty in this country and when their service was no longer needed on the Sumpter, the locomotives went on to additional glory in Central America.

The Baldwin Locomotive Works built the Sprague designed 2-6-6-2T locomotives for the Uintah Railway in 1926 and 1928. Baldwin's photographer made more than the usual builders photo record of these slim gauge giants, the largest ever built for domestic service. — H. L. BROAD-BELT COLLECTION

RICHARD KINDIG ON THE SUMPTER VALLEY AT 5° BELOW

Richard H. Kindig happened upon the Sumpter Valley Railway one cold December day in 1946 with Graflex in hand. The thermometer registered five degrees below zero as No. 251 blasted out of Baker, leaking steam as she went. With Hank Griffiths, the two rail photographers drove over icy backwoods roads pacing the little train. In one attempt to gain distance on the Mallet and her 21-car consist, their auto hit a patch of ice and turned completely around three times . . . afterwards the pace was a bit more leisurely. On the left, No. 251 beside the Austin water tank, while below she blasts across the snow-covered valley six miles south of Baker. On the opposite page, the westbound train rolls out of McEwen at 20 m.p.h. In the lower scene, the No. 251 returning in the afternoon with 15 loads of lumber.

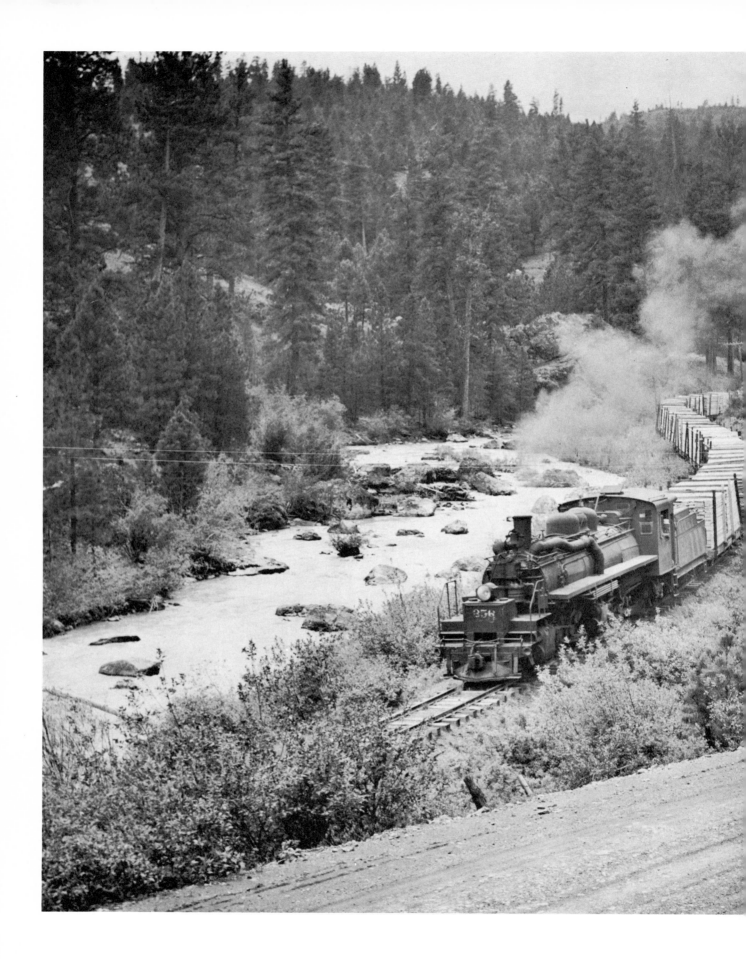

Dramatic and thundering is No. 250 as she swings her graceful 2-6-6-2 articulated frame around the S curve just east of Boulder Gourge on June 22, 1946, with 22 cars of cut lumber for Baker. — HENRY R. GRIFFITHS In the scene above, the first baby Mallet is captured on film during the closing years of World War II on a brief bit of straight track just west of Baker. — CHARLES M. CLEGG

The aromatic pungency of wood smoke, hot metal and valve oil fills the air near Salisbury, as No. 16 rolls a westbound train. — HENRY R. GRIFFITHS

FORM 55 SVR   SUMPTER VALLEY RAILWAY COMPANY

Station _Austin_   Date _8-5-40_

TRAIN REGISTER

EASTBOUND				WESTBOUND			
Train or Engine	Time Arrived	Time Departed	Conductor	Train or Engine	Time Arrived	Time Departed	Conductor
X250		7³⁵a	French	X250	9⁰⁰a		French
X16		12⁴⁰p	Rhea	X16	9⁴⁰		Rhea
X250		12¹⁰p	French	X251	12⁰⁷		Rug
X251		1⁰⁵	Rug	X250	5³⁰	tuch 6⁴³⁰	French

INSTRUCTIONS—Conductors must indicate time as called for hereon, and show time off duty in "Time Departed" column.
Agents will furnish new card each day and permanently file old cards in date order.

Surging over light rails, articulated No. 250 with a westbound
train of empties and mixed freight twists along the bank of the
Powder River in the last year of the road's glory. — AL FARROW

Against the backdrop of imposing Oregon countryside, No. 250 follows the trout-filled Powder River on its way to Baker. — AL FARROW In the scene below, No. 251 swings her train of stock cars through the wye at Tipton in 1946. Note how boiler swings out as the front engine rounds the sharp curve. — WARREN K. MILLER

END OF THE LINE — On April 11, 1947, the Sumpter Valley's final scheduled train from Bates heads eastbound along the Powder River near Boulder Gorge. — HENRY R. GRIFFITHS At the upper right, No. 251 and caboose 5 switch at Tipton during the last stock season for the Stump Dodger line. — WARREN K. MILLER No. 251 sends its exhaust towering above the trees as its mixed consist smokes into Salisbury at 35 miles per hour. — HENRY R. GRIFFITHS

The daily Stump Dodger ready for the morning run is seen above and at the upper right — AL FARROW At the right, transfer of mail and express is taking place at the Bates station. (Left) The daily mixed train. — MALLORY HOPE FERRELL COLLECTION

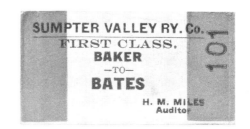

SUMPTER VALLEY RY. Co.
FIRST CLASS.
BAKER
—TO—
BATES
101
H. M. MILES
Auditor

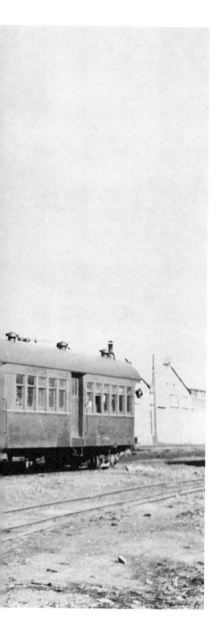

STUMP DODGER QUITS

The daily passenger train from Baker City was called the *Stump Dodger*. This varnish made its daily ramblings from Baker to Sumpter, then over the hills to Austin, Bates, Prairie City and returned via the same twisting route. The train normally departed at eight in the morning and was home before dinner. Conductor David Baird was an institution on the train and he held down the run for several decades. Dave would collect his tickets, then inquire who wished to eat in Austin. At S Wye he wired the expected number of dinners to the agent in Austin, who in turn passed the head count to "Ma" Austin. Later, when the new company town of Batesville was set up, passengers dined in the new town. After David Baird and Ma Austin's days, the train saw fewer and fewer passengers. The last run was made July 31, 1937, although passengers were allowed to ride the caboose up till the end of regular main line freight service.

MALLETS SOUTH OF THE BORDER

Photographed By Frank Barry

With the end of regular service on the Sumpter Valley Railway, the two former Uintah Mallets were once again homeless. This time they were sent south to Guatemala for duty on the narrow gauge International Railways of Central America.

The engines were assigned to IRCA's 3.7 per cent Palin Hill grade between Escuintla and Palin, on the Pacific escarpment. This grade consisting of 16 miles of unrelenting gradient in a series of loops, is one of the toughest in Central America. The Mallets proved too slippery on this grade, no doubt due to the weight loss when the side tanks were replaced by regular tenders.

No. 250 was overhauled and assigned to the Escuintla-Mazatenango local freight, a task she performed when these photographs were taken in 1962. The train ran on alternate days, working westbound on Tuesday, Thursday and Saturday and eastbound on Wednesday, Friday and Sunday. The terrain of Guatemala is lush and hilly along the Pacific coastal plain with short climbs of 2.2 per cent in both directions near Buena Vista and a 3.1 per cent grade approaching Escuintla.

At the right, No. 250 may be seen crossing the high bridge at Rio Coyolare with an eastbound freight during March 1962. *(Above)* Mallet meets the daily passenger train at Obispo. At the left, No. 250 labors out of Santa Maria on the 68-mile Mazatenango-Escuintla run.

A Union Pacific stock extra climbs the heavy grade out of Baker with a hefty 2-8-8-0 No. 3523 on the head end. A helper of the same class can be seen at the base of the snow covered Blue Mountains in the distance. *(Below)* The freight behind another 2-8-8-0 steams its way out of Baker yard with a pusher smoking alongside the Sumpter depot at the left. — HENRY R. GRIFFITHS

Union Pacific passenger trains were drawn into Baker behind such
machines as No. 800, a fast rolling 4-8-4. — HENRY R. GRIFFITHS

The Union Pacific main line connection was like an
artery for the narrow gauge Sumpter Valley. The
standard gauge was built through Baker City in 1884
as the Oregon Railway & Navigation Company, which
became part of the Oregon Short Line, a Union Pacific subsidiary three years later.

UNION PACIFIC – CONNECTION WITH THE WORLD

Baker, located in the middle of the Eastern Oregon
Division, was a helper station in steam days. It was
often called an operating nightmare since there were
two humps in the division extending from Huntington to La Grande with Baker in the middle. There
was plenty of action with helpers moving back over
the grades and regular trains rolling into town like
clockwork. The pace was intensified during the an-
nual stock season.

Sumpter switch engines had adjustable coupler poc-
kets for switching standard gauge cars on the dual
gauge tracks around Baker. Every shipment on the
narrow gauge destined for the "outside world" had
to be transferred to standard gauge cars at Baker,
such as the entire trainload of lumber at the left. —
HENRY R. GRIFFITHS

99

NOON-DAY WATER STOP

Photographed By Al Farrow

The Sumpter Valley erected their typical octagon shaped 9,000 gallon water tanks every few miles along the right-of-way . . . ten of them in all. The Mallets with their large tenders bypassed many tanks, but invariably paused at S Wye for a drink before battling the four per cent to Larch. No. 250 at the left passes the tank near Boulder Gorge. *(Below)* The 2-6-6-2 pauses for a fresh drink at S Wye before taking the first part of its train up the mountain. *(Top-Left)* The baby Mallet takes water at noontime after returning for the second half of its westbound train. It was often necessary to double the hill out of S Wye even with the Mallets. The view over some 35 empty flatcars was clear for the conductor aboard the caboose.

SUMPTER VALLEY RAILWAY COMPANY

S
V

TIME TABLE No. 59

Effective Saturday, June 13, 1936

AT 12:01 A. M. PACIFIC TIME

S
V

Journal box cover from No. 11, former Utah Northern 2-6-0, was cast by Union Pacific in the late 1870's. Passes and photos are reminders of bygone line down the valley.

CHAPTER 6

Nuts And Bolts

A HISTORY of the Sumpter Valley Railway and associated logging railroads would be incomplete without examination of the unique, but highly functional equipment in use on the narrow gauge. Tracing the travels of locomotives and rolling stock, largely second or thirdhand to begin with, was no easy task. This search led through wrecks, rebuildings, renumberings, trade, sale and scrappings, etc., and has taken years to compile. To build a roster of such a railroad as the Sumpter Valley, the author found the problem compounded by the lack of records, misleading transcriptions arranged to dismay the Utilities Commission, and with general renumberings that were not important enough at the time to register. Nevertheless, through the concerted efforts of several fellow rail historians and the last minute discovery of a 1909 official roster, we are able to present an accurate resume of the goings on at South Baker from beginning to end.

All of the early Sumpter Valley cars and most of the locomotives were obtained secondhand from the Union Pacific owned Utah & Northern Railway, which in July 1887, converted part of their Pocatello to Ogden mainline to standard gauge. By 1889, there were some 31 remaining narrow gauge locomotives on that line, then included as a part of the Union

Pacific's Oregon Short Line & Utah Northern. A few years later, only four narrow gauge locomotives remained, the balance having been sold to other short line railroads, logging lines, sugar refineries, and mining operations at a reported sale price of $150 each. The four narrow gauge teakettles were retained for service until 1902 on the Utah & Nevada Railway branch out of Salt Lake City.

Unfortunately all of the pre-1897 Oregon Short Line motive power records were contained in two 60-foot wooden baggage cars that were burned during a Union Pacific clean-up program many years ago.

The Sumpter Valley did not set up their first official roster until about 1893. Things went along pretty smoothly until 1906, which saw the arrival of four locomotives and a general renumbering of motive power. To compound the problem, the Oregon Public Service Commission was abolished by the legislature in 1897 and not re-established until 1906, resulting in a lack of records for those years.

The next major change in motive power came in 1912, when the Sumpter Valley Railway and the Eureka-Nevada Railway exchanged three locomotives in one of the most weird trades of the century. Neither railroad got much use out of their acquisition of antique engines.

Here then, we present the details of motive power and rolling stock for the edification of those interested in what Lucius Beebe once termed, "Nuts and Bolts."

	NO.	TYPE	BUILDER	C/N	DATE	DRI.	CYL.	WEIGH
	285	4-4-0	Baldwin	4982	1880	44	12x16	37,50
	1	2-6-0	Brooks	530	1881	42	14x18	45,80
2nd	1	2-6-0	Baldwin	19211	1901	44	16x20	81,29
	2	2-6-0	Brooks		1881	42	14x18	45,80
2nd	2	2-6-0	Baldwin	19210	1901	44	16x20	81,29
	3	2-6-0	Baldwin	5695	1881	41	14x18	47,00
2nd	3	2-8-0	Baldwin	9519	1888	38	16x20	82,08
	4	4-4-0	Baldwin	4982	1880	44	12x16	37,50
2nd	4	2-6-0	Baldwin	24689	1904	44	16x22	82,00
	5	2-6-0	Brooks	530	1881	42	14x18	45,80
	6	2-6-0	Brooks		1881	42	14x18	47,00
	7	2-8-0	Baldwin	5164	1880	36	15x18	54,00
2nd	7	2-6-0	Brooks		1881	42	14x18	45,80
	8	2-8-0	Baldwin	5930	1881	36	15x18	54,00
2nd	8	2-6-0	Brooks		1881	42	14x18	47,00
	9	2-6-0	Brooks		1881	42	14x18	47,00
	10	2-8-0	Baldwin	5164	1880	36	15x18	54,00
2nd	10	4-4-0	Baldwin	5285	1880	41	14x18	48,00
	11	2-6-0	Baldwin	4429	1878	40	12x18	39,00
2nd	11	2-8-0	Baldwin	5930	1881	36	15x18	54,00
	12	2-6-0	Brooks			42	14x18	45,80

Brooks built 2-6-0 was 1st No. 1 —
MALLORY HOPE FERRELL COLLECTION

Tonopah R.R. No. 1 became 2nd No.
1. — H. L. BROADBELT COLLECTION

No. 3 saw service on the Nevada-California-Oregon. — CLAUDE GREEN

Another Tonopah R.R. engine was
2nd No. 4. — BILL ROUNDY

RAILWAY

REMARKS

...ginal Utah Western 3 "Jonathan," Utah & Nevada 3 in 1881, to Oregon Short Line ...Utah Northern as 2nd No. 285 in 1888 (part of Union Pacific System). Became ...mpter Valley 285 in summer of 1890, renumbered 4, then 15. Became Eureka-Nevada ... in 1912 and scrapped.

...ginal Utah Northern 31, renumbered 88 in 1885, to Oregon Short line & Utah ...thern 88 in 1889. Became Sumpter Valley 1 in 1892, renumbered 5 in 1906. Traded ...ureka-Nevada, becoming their No. 5 in 1912. Rebuilt in 1919 and renumbered 9.

...ginal Chateaugay Ry. 16, to Tonopah Ry. as 2nd No. 1. Became Sumpter Valley 2nd ... 1 in 1906. Wrecked at Alder Springs in 1927. Retired 1934.

...ey 2, renumbered 2nd No. 7 in 1906. Scrapped in early 1930's.
...ginal Tonopah Railroad 4. Became Sumpter Valley 2nd No. 4 in 1906. Retired.

...ginal Chateaugay Ry. 15, to Tonopah Ry. as No. 2. Became Sumpter Valley 2nd ... 2 in 1906. Retired in 1930.

...ginal Minneapolis Lyndale & Minnetonka 13 "Dr. W. B. Hanks." Became Sumpter ...ey 3 about 1893, renumbered 13. Scrapped 1915.

...ginal Nevada-California-Oregon 4, became Tonopah Ry. 3. Became Sumpter Valley ... No. 3 in 1906. Retired 1930. Used by Oregon Lumber Co. in logging service.

...umbered from No. 285, later 1st No. 15.

...ginal Tonopah Railroad 4. Became Sumpter Valley 2nd No. 4 in 1906. Retired

Sumpter Valley No. 1.

...mer Oregon Short Line & Utah Northern. Became Sumpter Valley 6 in 1903.

...ginal Denver & Rio Grande 74 "Hermano," became D&RGW Ry. 74 in 1886, then Rio ...nde Western 74. Sold to Rio Grande Southern as No. 30 in 1891, became Rio ...nde Western No. 04 in 1899. Became Sumpter Valley 7 in 1900, renumbered 10. ... of service at Bates 4/24/24, on scrap line in 1936.

Sumpter Valley No. 2.

...ginal Connotton Valley Ry. 13 "Carrolton." Sold to New York Equipt. Co. in 1889. ...aired and sold to Utah Central. Rio Grande Western absorbed UC and renumbered ...No. 02, in 1898. Sold 1900 to Sumpter Valley becoming No. 8, renumbered 2nd No. 11. ...apped about 1914.

...mer Oregon Short Line & Utah Northern. Became Sumpter Valley 2nd No. 8 about ...3. Scrapped in the 1920's.

...mer OSL&UN. Became Sumpter Valley 9 about 1903. Scrapped between 1925-1930.

Sumpter Valley No. 7.

...ginal Carson & Colorado 1 "Candalaria." Sold 1907 to Eureka & Palisade for $2,500. ...ame Sumpter Valley 2nd No. 10 in 1912, and unsuitable for main line service. Used ...Oregon Lumber Co. as No. 103. Scrapped at Bates about 1936.

...ginal Utah Northern 7, renumbered 11, to OSL&UN 11 (used on Utah & Nevada ...air Line). Became Sumpter Valley 11 about 1902, renumbered 2nd No. 12 in 1906. ...sented to University of Idaho, scrapped in 1942.

Sumpter Valley No. 8.

...ner Utah Northern, and Oregon Short Line & Utah Northern. Shown in early Baker ... photograph.

Mudhen No. 14 came from the Eureka & Palisade. — SUMPTER COLLECTION

No. 8 was formerly Oregon Short Line & Utah Northern. — BRUCE MOREHEAD

No. 9 at Prairie City with the passenger. — ED HIBBS ALBUM

No. 15 in service on Eureka-Nevada Railway during 1912. — G. M. BEST

No. 16 was built new for the Sumpter Valley line. — WILLIAM BISSINGER

No. 18 was one of the three Baldwin built 2-8-2's. — JOHN B. ALLEN

No. 20 at Austin during the winter of 1939. — HENRY R. GRIFFITHS

No. 50 was used mostly for passenger service. — MAL FERRELL COLLECTION

	NO.	TYPE	BUILDER	C/N	DATE	DRI.	CYL.	WEIG
2nd	12	2-6-0	Baldwin	4429	1878	40	12x18	39,0
	13	2-6-0	Baldwin	5695	1881	41	14x18	47,0
	14	2-6-0	Baldwin		1882		14x18	47,0
2nd	14	2-8-0	Baldwin	28806	1906	38	16x22	94,8
	15	4-4-0	Baldwin	4982	1880	44	12x16	37,5
2nd	15	2-8-0	Baldwin	11075	1890	37	16x20	78,5
	16	2-8-2	Baldwin	42073	1915	42	17x22	141,9
	17	2-8-2	Baldwin	42074	1915	42	17x22	141,9
	18	2-8-2	Baldwin	42815	1916	42	17x22	141,9
	19	2-8-2	Schenectady	61981	1920	44	19x20	202,0
	20	2-8-2	Schenectady	61980	1920	44	19x20	202,0
	20	Railcar	White/Shops		1917			
	50	4-6-0	Baldwin	42865	1916	42	16x20	113,9
	100	0-4-0	Whitcomb	13015	1929			
	101	Shay	Lima	1884	1907	29	8x10	48,0
2nd	101	2-8-2	Schnectady	61980	1920	44	19x20	202,0
3rd	101	0-4-0	Davenport	2245	1937	30		60,0
	102	Shay	Lima	1885	1907	29	8x10	48,0
2nd	102	2-8-2	Schenectady	61981	1920	44	19x20	202,0
	250	2-6-6-2	Baldwin	59261	1926	42	15x22	185,0
	251	2-6-6-2	Baldwin	60470	1928	42	15x22	190,0

NOTE: In some cases engine weight may differ from Baldwin Locomotive Works or Bro records. Such weights were obtained from the 1909 Oregon Railroad Commiss Appraisal of the Sumpter Valley and figures include the addition of air brak automatic couplers and modifications not on the locomotive as built at locomotive builder.

RAILWAY

REMARKS

e Sumpter Valley No. 11.

e Sumpter Valley No. 3.

rchased secondhand from Oregon Short Line about 1903. Traded to Eureka-Nevada
1912.

rmer Eureka & Palisade 8. Became Sumpter Valley 2nd No. 14 in 1912. Retired 1931.

e Sumpter Valley No. 285.

iginal Alberta Ry. & Coal Co. 7. Sold to Eureka & Palisade at time of 1910 washouts
d not used. In 1912 Eureka-Nevada traded engine to Sumpter Valley as their 2nd No.
. Retired in 1921.

quired new. Originally a woodburner, converted to oil in 1940. Retired in August 1944.
ld to Peruvian Government in 1945.

quired new. Same note as No. 16.

quired new. Retired January 1943. Same note as No. 16.

quired new. Originally No. 102, renumbered 19. Retired 1940 and sold to White Pass
Yukon as their No. 81.

quired new. Originally No. 101, renumbered 20. Retired 1940 and sold to White Pass
Yukon as their No. 80.

ilt in Sumpter Valley shops from a White Motor Co. truck body. Had 4-wheel lead
ick, 2-wheel power truck. Carried 27 passengers. Wrecked shortly after placed in
rvice and scrapped.

quired new. Retired December 1941. Sold to Peruvian Government in 1945.

s mechanical switcher. Former Shirley Construction Co., Yale & Regan Co. 8. Became
mpter Valley 100 during April 1930.

quired new. Owned by Oregon Lumber Co., but originally lettered Sumpter Valley.
e Oregon Lumber Co. roster.

e Sumpter Valley No. 20.

esel mechanical switcher. Acquired new. Sold to Denver & Rio Grande Western as
eir No. 50 in 1963. Used as switcher at Durango, Colorado.

cquired new. Owned by Oregon Lumber Co., but originally lettered Sumpter Valley. See
regon Lumber Co. roster.

e Sumpter Valley No. 19.

iginal Uintah Ry. 50. Became Sumpter Valley 250 during June 1940. Converted to oil
rner, saddle tanks removed and tender added. Retired 1947 and sold to Hyman-
chaels Co. a scrap dealer. Sold to International Railway of Central America, shipped
ly 1947.

iginal Uintah Ry. 51. Became Sumpter Valley 251 during June 1940. See Sumpter
lley No. 250 notes.

Shay No. 101 lettered for the Sumpter
Valley Railway. — FERRELL COLL.

American Locomotive Co. builders
shot of No. 101. — DON H. ROBERTS

Davenport diesel mechanical switcher
at Baker. — CHANDLER COLLECTION

Baldwin built 2-6-6-2 originally from
the Uintah Railway. — BERT WARD

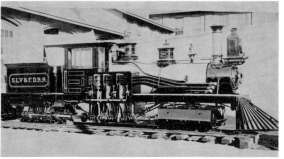

Oregon Lumber No. 1 as built by the Lima Works. — P. E. PERCY

Shay No. 7 first ran on the New Mexico Lumber Co. — FERRELL COLL.

Oregon Lumber Co. Heisler No. 100 at Batesville. — JOHN R. CUMMINGS

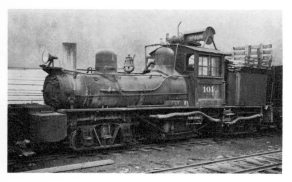

Oregon Lumber Co. No. 101 formerly Sumpter power. — EMERY J. ROBERTS

OREGON LUMBE

	NUMBER	TYPE	BUILDER	BUILDERS NO.	DATE	WEIG
	1	Shay	Lima	226	1888	40,
2nd	1	Shay	Lima	1983	1907	48,
	7	Shay	Lima	3345	1929	134,
	100	Heisler	Heisler	1510	1924	100,
	101	Shay	Lima	1884	1907	48,
	102	Shay	Lima	1885	1907	48,
	103	Shay	Lima	1983	1907	48,
2nd	103	4-4-0	Baldwin	5285	1880	48,
3rd	103	Heisler	Heisler	1184	1910	
	104	Heisler	Heisler	1188	1910	84,C
	105	Climax	Climax	1533	1919	60,C

STODDARD LUMB

	NUMBER	TYPE	BUILDER	BUILDERS NO.	DATE	WEIG
	1	Shay	Lima	224	1889	24,C
2nd	1	Climax	Climax	1077	1911	66,C
	2	Heisler	Heisler	1023	1898	50,C

108

PANY (1900-1943)

HISTORY/NOTES

uck, 20-ton, B-type woodburner. Built for Salt Lake Valley & Fort Douglas RR as their
226, became Utah Central Ry. 226 in 1890. Sold to Oregon Lumber Co. in 1893.
d 1920 to McKim & Co. a dealer.

uck, 24-ton, B-type. Renumbered to 103. Scrapped 20 miles from Baker during
uary 1927, following a wreck.

uck, 67-ton, C-type. Original New Mexico Lumber Co. 7. Became Oregon Lumber
7 in 1936. Was a woodburner, converted to oil by Sumpter Valley shops in 1941.
urned to woodburner in 1951. Sold to Black Hills Central RR as their No. 7 in 1962.
 assigned No. 107 by Oregon Lumber Co., but never so numbered on the locomotive.

uck, 50-ton, outside frame trucks. Purchased new for $18,055. Scrapped 1954.

uck, 24-ton, B-type. Ordered by David Eccles and lettered Sumpter Valley Railway.
t $12,400. Out of service at Bates in 1941 and scrapped.

uck, 24-ton, B-type. See notes above. Idle by 1941. Sold in 1945 to McKim & Son,
er, Oregon (dealer). Engine scrapped, boiler to Eagle Cap Laundry, Enterprise, Oregon,
946.

Oregon Lumber Co. 2nd No. 1.

Sumpter Valley 2nd No. 10. Renumbered to 103. Scrapped at Bates in 1936.

ick. Originally Moore Timber Co. 1, purchased by W. H. Eccles Lumber Co. from
der in 1916 as No. 2. Renumbered by Oregon Lumber Co. to No. 103.

ick, 42-ton. Built as standard gauge for Nibley Lumber Co's. Hilgard Lumber Co.
t Meacham, Oregon, for service on Blue Mountain RR, became Nibley-Nimnaugh
ber Co. 2, C. W. Nibley Lumber Co. 2 (Whitney, Oregon). Became Oregon Lumber
104 about 1915. Engine converted to 36-inch gauge at Sumpter Valley Shops 1911-
2. Scrapped at Baker in 1947.

ick, 30-ton, B-type. Original Hallack & Howard Lumber Co. 6 (LaMadera, New
ico). Became Oregon Lumber Co. 105. Scrapped 1949.

MPANY (1897-1943)

ick, 12-ton, A-type. Original Sunny South Lumber Co. 1., New Lewisville, Arkansas.
ght by Sumpter Valley in 1897 for Stoddard Brother Lumber as their No. 1. Known
Old Betsy." Scrapped December 1924.

ick, 33-ton, B-type. Former Baker White Pine 1, became Stoddard Lumber 2nd
1 in 1929. Srcapped.

ick, 25-ton. Original Blue Jay Lumber Co. 3, Sand Patch, Pa., became Stoddard
ber Co. 2 in 1903. Known as "Old Brigham." Scrapped in 1920's.

Oregon Lumber Co. No. 102 was idle
by 1941. — EMERY J. ROBERTS

Heisler No. 104 was built for standard
gauge use. — FERRELL COLL.

Oregon Lumber Co. Climax No. 105.
— T. G. WURM COLLECTION

Oregon Lumber No. 105 as built for
Halleck & Howard. — WALTER CASLER

Stoddard Heisler No. 3 at Baker mill pond. — WARREN E. MILLER

Stoddard Heisler No. 4 at Baker in 1947. — MAL FERRELL COLLECTION

No. 3 as built by the Heisler Locomotive Works. — CASLER COLLECTION

Builders photograph of Heisler No. 4. — BROOKS HAWLEY COLLECTION

STODDARD LUMBE

NUMBER		TYPE	BUILDER	C/N	DATE	WEIGH
2nd	2	Climax	Climax	1199	1913	90,0
	3	Heisler	Heisler	1360	1917	72,0
2nd	3	Climax	Climax	1355	1915	90,0
	4	Heisler	Heisler	1460	1922	80,0
	5	Heisler	Heisler	1360	1917	72,0

BAKER WHITE PINE L

	1	Climax	Climax	1077	1911	66,0
	2	Climax	Climax	1199	1913	70,0
	3	Climax	Climax	1355	1915	90,0

CAVANAUGH LUM

	3	Climax	Climax	1085	1911	64,0

C. W. NIBLEY LUM

	2	Heisler	Heisler	1188	1910	84,0

W. H. ECCLES LUM

	1	Climax	Climax	1085	1911	64,0
	2	Heisler	Heisler	1184	1910	
	3	Heisler	Heisler	1306	1915	80,0

PANY (1897-1943)

REMARKS

ruck, 35-ton, B-type. Former Baker White Pine 2, became Stoddard Lumber 2nd No. 2
1929. Scrapped.

ruck, 36-ton. Acquired new. Renumbered 5 when three Climax locomotives received
m Baker White Pine. Scrapped 1947.

ruck, 45-ton, B-type. Former Baker White Pine 3, became Stoddard Lumber 2nd No. 3
1929. Scrapped.

ruck, 40-ton. Acquired new. Scrapped in 1947.

Stoddard Lumber Co. No. 3.

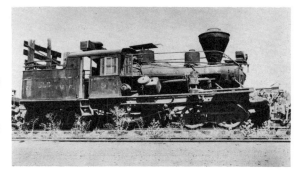

Stoddard Heisler No. 5 on the scrap
line in 1947. — MENDENHALL COLL.

COMPANY (1912-1929)

ruck, 33-ton, B-type. Acquired new. Became Stoddard Lumber 2nd No. 1 in 1929

ruck, 35-ton, B-type. Acquired new. Became Stoddard Lumber 2nd No. 2 in 1929.

ruck, 45-ton, B-type. Acquired new. Become Stoddard Lumber 2nd No. 3 in 1929.

Scene at the Bates yard of Oregon
Lumber. — MAL FERRELL COLLECTION

MPANY (1929-1931)

uck, 32-ton, B-type. Original W. H. Eccles Lumber 1, became Cavanaugh Lumber 3
1929. Sold to Oregon Lumber in 1931, but never used. Scrapped.

MPANY (1911-1915)

uck, 42-ton. See Oregon Lumber No. 104.

Baker White Pine Climax No. 1. —
BROOKS HAWLEY COLLECTION

MPANY (1911-1926)

uck, 32-ton, B-type. Acquired new. Sold to Cavanaugh Lumber as their No. 3 in
9. Became Oregon Lumber property in 1931, but never used.

uck. Original Moore Timber 1, sold to W. H. Eccles Lumber by Heisler in 1916. Became
gon Lumber 103 in 1926.

uck, 40-ton. Acquired new. Operated in Baker region until late 1920's. Sold to
ack & Howard Lumber, Cascade, Idaho, as their No. 3. Still in shed at Cascade
red W. H. Eccles Lbr. Co., now owned by Boise-Cascade Corporation.

Cavanaugh Lumber Co. Climax No. 1
at Austin. — BERT WARD COLLECTION

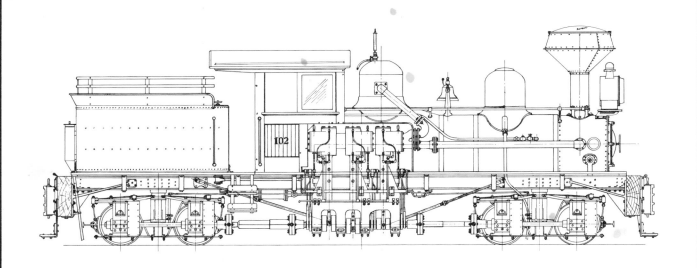

OREGON LUMBER COMPANY
SHAY LOCOMOTIVE NO. 102

Drawn by H. Temple Crittenden
Scale: 3/16″ = 1′-0″

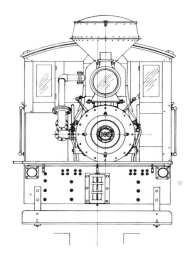

Oregon Lumber Company's Shay Locomotive No. 102 was built by the Lima Locomotive Works in 1907 as construction No. 1884. This engine cost $12,400 to construct and came lettered for the Sumpter Valley Railway and was identical to No. 101 built at the same time. The two-truck Shay weighed 48,500 pounds, had three 8x10-inch cylinders, 29-inch drivers and in general was a typical Shay geared engine of the period. The little sidewinder later had a yarding winch added to her front pilot, and saw other changes like a new cab and tank due to being rolled over on several occasions in logging work. She was completely wrecked in 1912 on Mosquito Creek below Whitney. Here she ran away on a little used spur in the process of being removed and killed a section hand. The Shay was idle by 1941 and sold to the Eagle Cap Laundry of Enterprise, Oregon, in 1946.

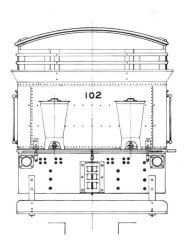

Caboose No. 5 on the end of a train at Baker during the last years of Sumpter Valley operation.—WARREN MILLER

SUMPTER VALLEY RAILWAY
CABOOSE CAR NO. 5

Drawn by H. Temple Crittenden
Scale: 3/16″ = 1′-0″

Caboose No. 5 was constructed in the South Baker Shops during the autumn of 1926. The car was rebuilt from parts obtained from a caboose of Utah & Northern heritage. The author has an iron journal box cover from this car cast by the Union Pacific for its narrow gauge Utah Northern prior to April 1878, when the road became the Utah & Northern. This caboose was similar in design and construction to cabooses Nos. 3, 4 and 6. It was painted in grey livery and trimmed in black around windows and underframe.

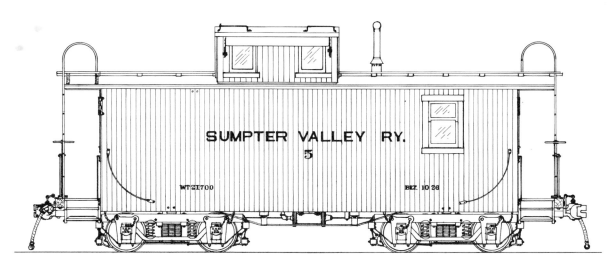

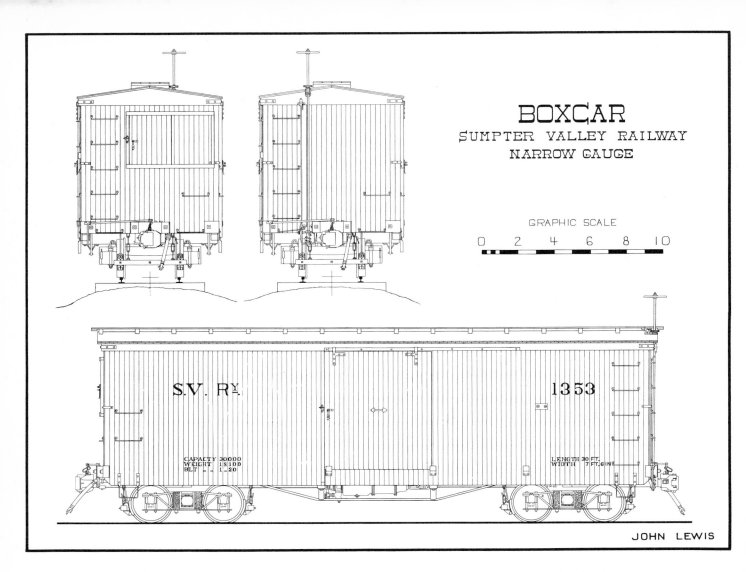

BOXCAR
SUMPTER VALLEY RAILWAY
NARROW GAUGE

GRAPHIC SCALE

0   2   4   6   8   10

S.V. Rʸ.   1353

CAPACITY 30000
WEIGHT 18100   LENGTH 30 FT.
BLT _ _ 1 _20   WIDTH   7 FT.6 IN.

JOHN LEWIS

The Sumpter Valley had a variety of wooden boxcars and No. 1351 is typical of the road. Note the wood bolstered arch bar trucks. — HENRY R. GRIFFITHS

Flatcar No. 76638 on a siding in Baker. — F. M. CHANDLER COLLECTION (*Lower-Left*) Bettendorf freight car trucks as used on this class of flatcar. — J. R. CUMMINGS COLLECTION (*Lower-Right*) Flatcar side and end details. — IVAN ERGISH

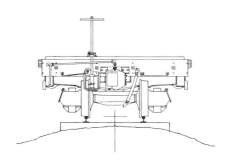

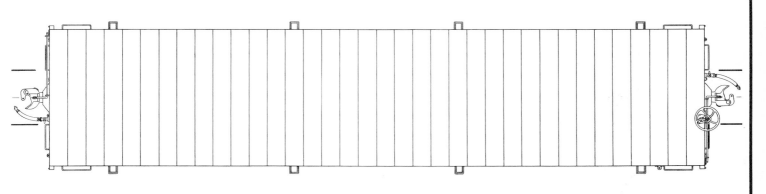

FLATCAR
SUMPTER VALLEY RAILWAY
NARROW GAUGE

GRAPHIC SCALE

0   2   4   6   8   10

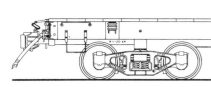

S.V.RY. 76605

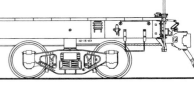

JOHN LEWIS

Sumpter Valley 2000 series stockcar. — HENRY R. GRIFFITHS

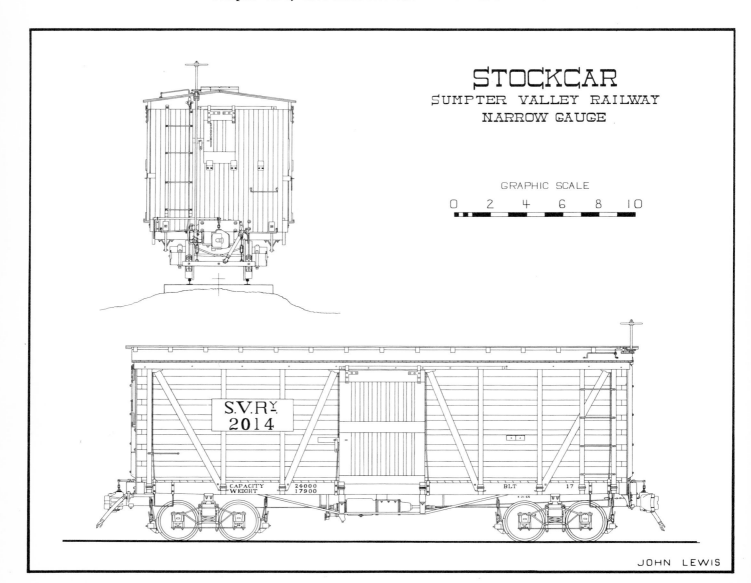

STOCKCAR
SUMPTER VALLEY RAILWAY
NARROW GAUGE

GRAPHIC SCALE

0   2   4   6   8   10

S.V.Ry.
2014

CAPACITY   24000
WEIGHT   17900

BLT   17

JOHN LEWIS

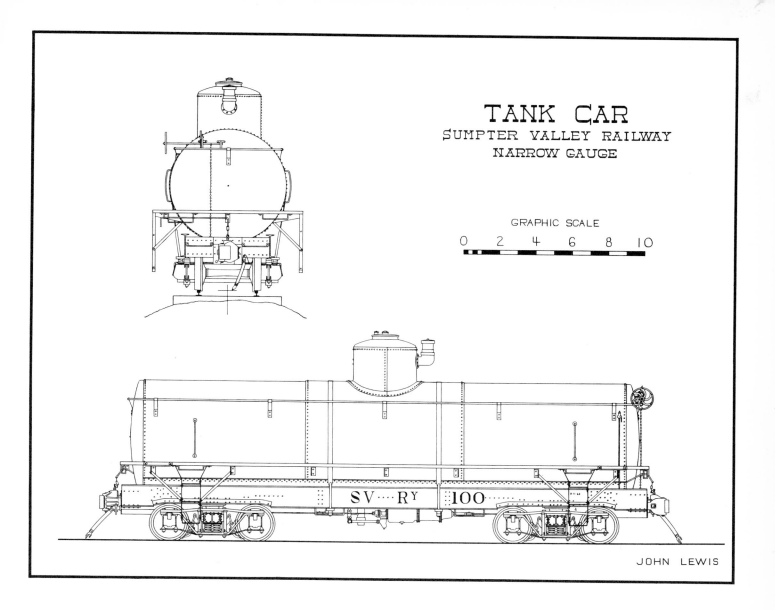

TANK CAR
SUMPTER VALLEY RAILWAY
NARROW GAUGE

GRAPHIC SCALE

0   2   4   6   8   10

SV · RY 100

JOHN LEWIS

Sumpter Valley 6,500 gallon capacity tank car at Baker. — WARREN MILLER (*Below*) The tank car truck. — IVAN ERGISH

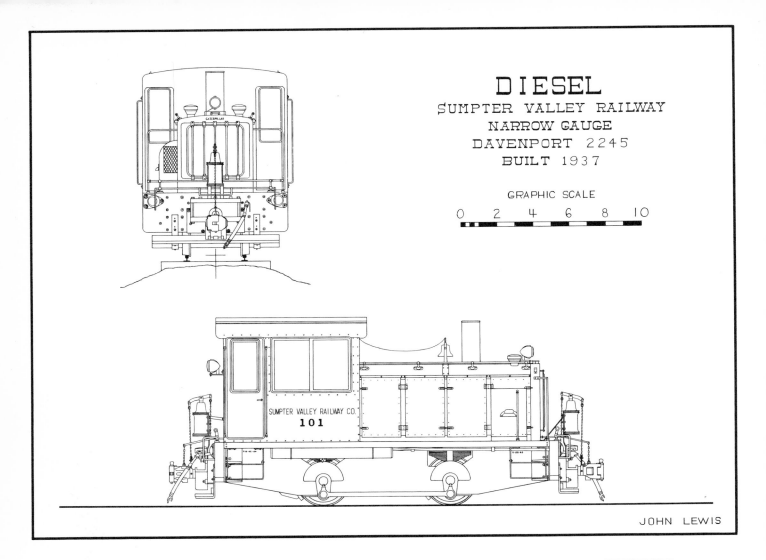

DIESEL
SUMPTER VALLEY RAILWAY
NARROW GAUGE
DAVENPORT 2245
BUILT 1937

GRAPHIC SCALE

0   2   4   6   8   10

SUMPTER VALLEY RAILWAY CO.
101

JOHN LEWIS

Diesel mechanical switcher built by Davenport in 1937
and equipped with a Caterpillar engine. — FRED JUKES

Sumpter dump car on a siding in Baker. Note the link n' pin coupler. — WARREN MILLER

Gondola ore car No. 102 was used during quartz mining days on the Sumpter Valley. — TED WURM

At one time the Sumpter Valley possessed a considerable fleet of fine passenger equipment. Only three cars were in serviceable condition up to the end of service. These distinctive "turtle-back" cars built wholly of wood were heated by small coal stoves, one in each end, with kerosene lamps hanging from the ceiling, and seats covered in cane. In the view above, passenger train No. 1 waits beside the Bates sawmill while crew clear a frozen switch. — MIKE WELTER At the right, the interior of car No. 26, long after the abandonment of passenger service. — LAWTON GOWEY

Car No. 4 was distinctly a different car in length and interior appointments. It had a separate mail section and baggage compartment.—RAY BUHRMASTER

As originally supplied by the builders, Nos. 25 and 26 were identical day coaches. No. 26 was later sent to the shops and converted into a combination car through the installation of two side doors, one on either side near the end. Later a second compartment was built-in with a door on each side. At the right, No. 25 at Baker. — HENRY R. GRIFFITHS The lower view shows car No. 26 after the second rebuilding. — RICHARD KINDIG

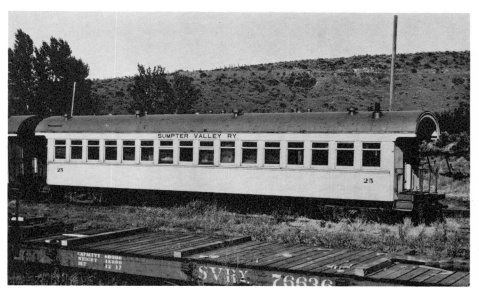

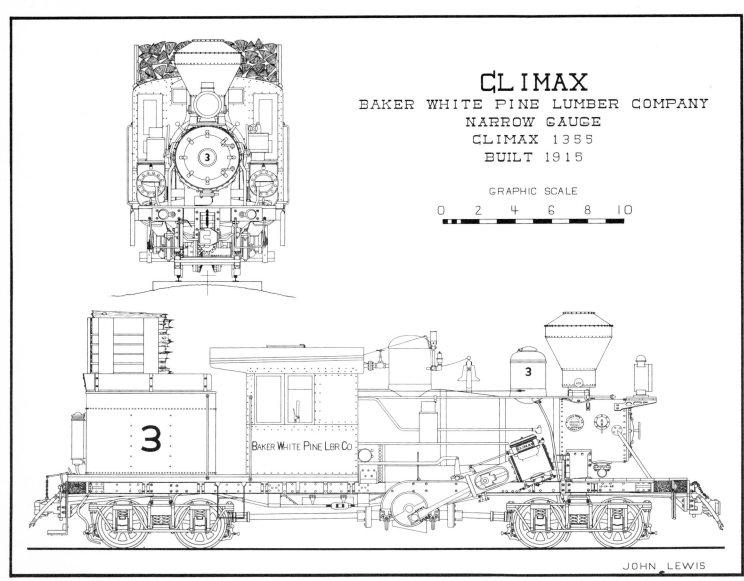

CLIMAX
BAKER WHITE PINE LUMBER COMPANY
NARROW GAUGE
CLIMAX 1355
BUILT 1915

GRAPHIC SCALE

0   2   4   6   8   10

3

BAKER WHITE PINE LBR CO

JOHN LEWIS

Baker White Pine Climax No. 3 as photographed at the Climax plant in Corry, Pennsylvania. This 2-truck, 45-ton, B-type locomotive was the heaviest on the line.
— **WALTER CASLER**

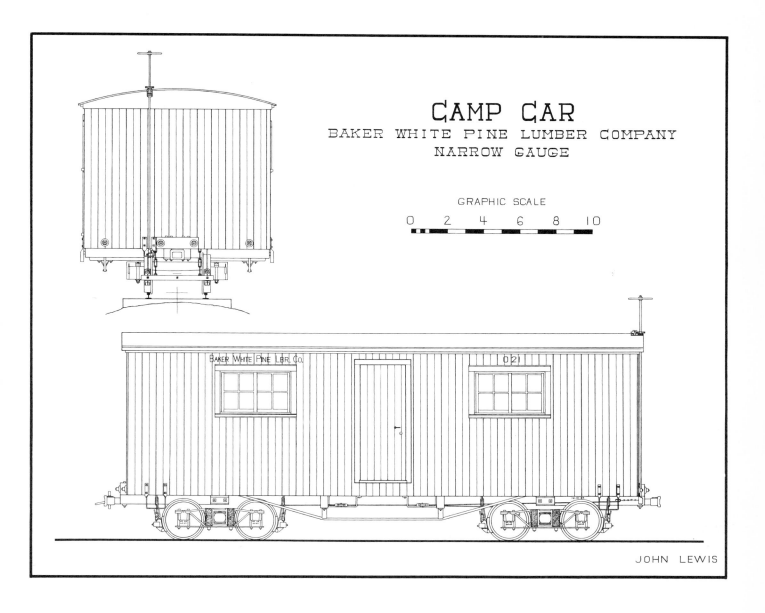

CAMP CAR
BAKER WHITE PINE LUMBER COMPANY
NARROW GAUGE

GRAPHIC SCALE

0   2   4   6   8   10

JOHN LEWIS

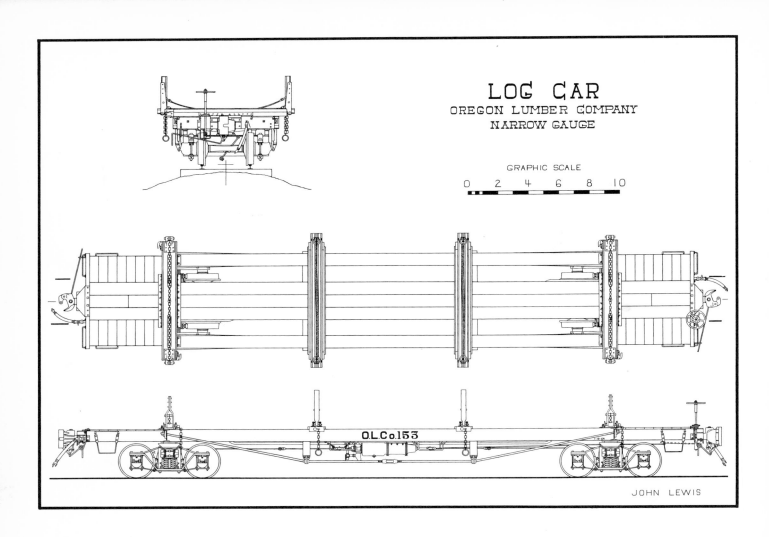

LOG CAR
OREGON LUMBER COMPANY
NARROW GAUGE

GRAPHIC SCALE

0   2   4   6   8   10

O.L.Co.153

JOHN LEWIS

Oregon Lumber log cars were a modified Skelton type car with a bunk over each truck and two additional bunks in the center portion. Extra chocks prevented the bottom tier of logs from rolling off. Note the extra braces and truss rods added to the car for strength. — BOTH F. M. CHANDLER

The stations along the Sumpter Valley Railway were not impressive like the short line itself. The Baker station was typical of any Western depot scene. The trackside illustration covers Baker rail facilities with the Sumpter Valley station on the left and the main line Union Pacific depot directly across the tracks to the right.

(Left) Dual gauge yard tracks at Baker. — LUCIUS BEEBE *(Center)* The Sumpter main line passing through Austin, complete with water tank and engine shed at the left. *(Right)* The Sumpter's tracks should not be confused with the Union Pacific main line! Not all trackage was surface bent like this section west of Baker.

Baker yard in April 1947, shortly after the last run. The engine house is at the left with Sumpter Valley and Oregon Lumber Co. equipment stored on sidings. — MALLORY HOPE FERRELL *(Right)* S Wye with the main line coming in from Whitney. At the wye, Baker was to the right and Sumpter to the left. — HENRY R. GRIFFITHS

Sagebrush and pine reclaim their own. — MALLORY HOPE FERRELL

Index

Golden West Books

P.O. Box 8136 · San Marino, California · 91108